When Waterford & I Were Young

Teresa & Bob

John can't sign this book I know he wants you as very dear friends to have it

Bonnie Mc Divine

John E. Divine
(1911-1996)

with

Bronwen C. Souders
John M. Souders

1997

> *For*
> "Mac," Lynn, and Nancy

Copyright ©1997
Waterford Foundation, Inc.
Waterford, Virginia

ISBN No. 0-9660485-2-0 hardbound
ISBN No. 0-9660485-1-2 paperback

Library of Congress Catalogue Card Number: 97-61707

No part of this book may be reproduced or used in any form without the express permission of the publisher in writing.

Printed by Bookcrafters, Inc., Fredericksburg, Virginia

> *Cover: John Divine with friend Buster in front of the Mahlon Janney house on Main Street Hill, about 1915.*

PREFACE

At his death in November 1996, John Divine had enjoyed a full and fruitful eighty-five years as a soldier, citizen, businessman, husband and father. But most who were privileged to know him remember best his abiding interest in the history and people of his native Loudoun County, Virginia. His generous spirit and contagious enthusiasm wonderfully complemented his skill and discipline as a self-taught historian. This happy combination won him many disciples and—especially for his contributions to Civil War scholarship—national recognition.

It was his birthplace of Waterford, Virginia, that kindled John Divine's interest in history; he was the sixth generation of his family to make his home in that place. And it was to the 260-year-old village that his attention returned in the final years of his life. Persuaded by friends and family that his personal reminiscences and carefully preserved accounts of his forbears' village were treasures worth sharing, he agreed at last to commit them to paper.

This book is the result of that resolve. Although he did not live to complete it, he left a rich personal memoir. As a longtime friend and student, I have rounded out his anecdotes and added a bit of context (and surely a few errors), assisted immeasurably by my husband John. But the account is John Divine's. This book then stands both as his memorial to Waterford—its people and their times—and, in a small way, as our tribute to him.

He would not want me to close without acknowledging at least a few of the many people who helped with this book, especially Waterford natives Emma Myers, Gladys Jackson Lewis, Peggy Chalmers Pancoast, Emerson James, and Francis O. Peacock. Taylor Chamberlin provided a wealth of primary material as did Louisa Hutchison and Phebe Haviland Steer. Finally, the most indispensable partner in this project has been Bernice "Mac" Divine, John's wife of nearly fifty years and my tireless host. Thank you all.

Bronwen C. Souders
Waterford, Virginia
1997

This book is an authorized publication of the Waterford Foundation, Inc. The village and setting of Waterford, Virginia, were designated a National Historic Landmark in 1970 by the United States Department of the Interior. The Waterford Foundation is a non-profit organization dedicated to the preservation and interpretation of this unique national resource. All proceeds from the sale of this book are applied to that objective.

For more information about Waterford and the Foundation, write Waterford Foundation, Post Office Box 142, Waterford, VA 20197, or telephone (540) 882-3018.

Contents

Preface	3
Illustrations	6
Introduction	8
Still Waters	11
Founded by Friends	13
Fairfax Meeting	17
Janney's Mill	19
Development of Main Street	42
The Other Side of Main Street	54
The Town Council	63
Town Center	68
War Stories	77
A Few More War Stories	79
Ghosts	85
The Town Triangle & Big Hill	87
Cold—Good & Bad	94
New Town & The Industrial South End	97
Horsepower	114
Church Life	123
School Days	127
Postscript	136
Notes	137
Bibliography	139
Index	141

ILLUSTRATIONS

Maps

Janney & Hague Tracts	14
Mill, Tanyard & Bond Street	22
Main Street	29
New Town & South End	96

Other Illustrations

John E. Divine in 1984	9
Betsy Dodd Divine	10
Five Quakers of Fairfax Meeting	13
Fairfax Meeting House	19
Mill & millrace	20
Mill wheel	22
Advertisement for Quakertown Flour	22
Mill owners	22
Team & wagon at the scales	24
Personal estate of Francis Hague	30
Mill End	31
Hillside and mill storage building	33
John Wesley Church congregation	37
North end of village from 1882 sketch	41
Dan Walker & Old Bob	42
Log house of Ed Gaskins/Dan Walker	43
Canoers on millrace	46
Waterford bank note	48
Laura Page house	49
Theodore Mallory house	51
Sally Nettle house	52
Ratcliffe house	54
Kitty Leggett house & neighbors	56
Collins house	57

Marietta Collins	58
Arch House row	61
Town center, *circa* 1915	67
Johnson's Corner	70
Medicine show entertainers	71
Doc White & Robert B. Hough	73
View up Water Street & Main Street Hill, *circa* 1910	74
Old Corner Store	75
L.P. Smith letterhead	76
Joseph T. Divine	77
Fairfax Meeting House interior	80
Loudoun Rangers reunion	83
Sgt. Joseph T. Divine	84
Lloyd Curtis	90
John Divine on Main Street Hill	90
Mahlon Janney house	91
View down Main Street hill	92
Schooley's Mill	96
The Dormers	99
Old Acre	101
James M. Steer's cold iron works (diagram)	102
William Williams	105
Horse & driver on Second Street	104
Sunnyside	107
Doctors' House	110
E.L. James letterhead	111
Tin Shop	112
Ed Beans & wife	115
Lewis N. Hough chair/undertaking advertisement	122
Methodist Church picnickers fording Balls Run	124
Students at school on Second Street	128
Waterford Academy	129
Presbyterian Church and manse	133
James Lewis House	134

INTRODUCTION

The small Virginia town of John Divine's youth was the kind of place in which many of us would love to have grown up: long summers of swimming, fishing, and baseball, then the familiar regimens of church and school, the self-sufficiency of a community that produced its own food, built its own homes, looked after its own people. John remembered the women who raised turkeys for pocket money and put up their own vegetables for the winter. Even that harsh season had its attractions for the children who helped the men cut pond ice to fill the ice houses or sledded the third of a mile down the "Big Hill" to the mill.

As John matured, however, he was increasingly intrigued with his family's stories of early Waterford—of the old Quakers and Baptists, Presbyterians and Methodists, and of the sons of slaves and of free African Americans who had settled Waterford or spent time there. He realized that Waterford's experience was at once common to many Southern villages of his time and yet also remarkable. Life unfolded there in a particular, documentable way, molded at times by powerful outside forces while preserving a rare continuity. And he had been there and been a part of it.

In the early 1960s, after he had gone away to serve in World War II, returned, married, started a career and family, John began, on lunch hours and weekends, a detailed study of the village, right back to its roots as a part of the Northern Neck grant of King Charles II. Beginning with the help of neighbor and friend Ebenezer "Ebbie" Rollison, he painstakingly compiled notebooks of names, deed transactions, court cases, family relationships and the like. A natural historian, John was not satisfied with just facts, though he recorded and sourced all he could find, but in the who and how and why that gave them meaning.

One could hand John the 1820 Waterford census or a Civil War letter or an 1870 auction bill of sale, and have him say, for example, "*Well, Lewis Coale...now he was one of the first councilmen of the village, I've got that document here....*," and he would disappear into his library for a few moments and emerge with a copy of the appropriate corroborating record. A lively anecdote almost always accompanied the dry facts. As he explained to a fellow historian a few years ago, *"My great interest is in people and in human-interest stories."*

This book shares that human side of a special southern village, one founded in the 18th century on Quaker principles, then torn in the 1860s between Unionist sympathizers and secessionist partisans. It was a town whose commercial life flourished then slowly waned after that war. Finally, in 1970, it became a National Historic Landmark, not because anyone famous was born there, but because the village and its pastoral setting are so strongly evocative of America's past.

John's own memories of Waterford and its times spanned more than 80 years; the five generations of his family who preceded him there extended his personal ties in the area to the mid-1700s. Thus, he better than anyone can show us old Waterford, a place of contrasts that historian Edward Ayers has described so well, *"...a Quaker village in a Protestant area, a commercial center in an agricultural setting, and a haven for free African-Americans in a slave state."*[1]

JOHN DIVINE at Civil War Round-Table, Richmond, Virginia, 1984

ELIZABETH DODD DIVINE (1787-1874) knitting in the morning sun in Waterford, probably in the late 1860s. Betsy was the second wife of Jacob Divine, the author's great-great-grandfather. Her house on Bond Street has long since vanished; only a few tumbled stones mark the foundation. Virgin's Bower, a fragrant white-flowered clematis still common to Waterford fencerows, frames the scene.

Still Waters

In February 1888 an anonymous resident summed up his village for readers of the old *Loudoun Telegraph*.

> *WATERFORD IS QUIET—*
>
> *Socially there is nothing brilliant; the men attend the Farmers Club, the ladies go to their Household, both take a hand in an occasional quilting and the young folks hang over the front gate in the moonlight. Financially there is nothing startling. The several stores seem to be doing a fairly good business and the Mills seem to be quite busy but ready cash is not abundant. Religiously, the Town is experiencing no sensation at this time. Morally, there is occasion for the remark that Waterford is too near "The Point [of Rocks]" for its own good. In other towns of the County I hear the charge that there is a good deal of drinking in Waterford—and I am afraid the town is not in position to bring suit for slander on this score....*

Hardly a place to stir a reader's interest it would seem. But, considered over a longer span, the village has seen its share of memorable times—as well as a number that might better be forgotten.

So, if the venerable *Telegraph* has not sent you hurrying elsewhere for edification, I propose to share the good and the bad of old Waterford as my family and I knew it for some two hundred years. From peaceable Quakers to bloody battles, from progress and prosperity to flood and plague, from panthers to plumbing, from slaves to students, from old-fashioned "family values" to "fornication," demon rum, and murder. And if the going gets too heavy, I'll try to throw in enough recollected fun and foibles to tide us over the hard times.

Readers are forewarned that this memoir rambles over time and place. By and large it begins at the beginning, in the oldest part of the village, and follows the growth of the town. Inevitably, many worthy people, places, and events are bypassed, sometimes out of pure ignorance. Readers are earnestly invited to help fill in the gaps.

I admit to editorializing once or twice on the wider significance of local happenings. Take these opinions or leave them as you like. For the most part, though, I have set out the facts unvarnished; like Waterford itself they usually look better without embellishment.

Those Who Came First

For thousands of years before there was a Waterford the broad fertile valley between the Catoctin and Blue Ridge Mountains was the domain of the original Americans. They hunted its hills and fished its creeks. By some accounts they routinely burned over large areas to encourage the grasslands the deer and bison favored. But these people lived more lightly on the land than their successors and left few permanent marks of their long tenure. Aside from the stone points and other implements that farmers still turn up today, there is little more than place names to remind of their passage.

In 1722, after years of prodding by colonial authorities, the various tribes agreed to remain west of the Blue Ridge and north of the Potomac River. This Treaty of Albany opened the Loudoun Valley to European settlement. Most of the newcomers came from the north rather than from Tidewater Virginia. The first to arrive in numbers were German-speakers who established themselves just south of the Potomac. Quakers from Pennsylvania and New Jersey soon followed. They pressed beyond the German Settlement, as it came to be known, and took up land along Catoctin and Goose Creeks.

FOUNDED BY FRIENDS

By the time I came along in 1911, most of the Quakers in Waterford had long since died, moved on, or strayed from the faith—only a handful kept the old ways, and most of those were well along in years. But these were the people who first settled the place so long ago and who gave it much of the physical and social character that holds our interest today. They certainly made an impression on me growing up. So it seems fitting to begin any account of the village with the Quakers and the two most prominent landmarks they left—the mill and the meetinghouse.

Five Quakers of Fairfax Meeting (circa 1890)[2]

ANN T. GOVER (1820-1896), Sarah G. Janney White (1815-1905), Hannah Mendenhall Worley (c.1820-   ), Rachel Louisa (Lucy) Steer Schooley (1825-1896), Rachel Steer (1814-1912), lower right, the only face identified.

Waterford's pioneering Quakers were Amos and Mary Yardley Janney from Bucks County, Pennsylvania, north of Philadelphia. In the early 1680s the Janney and Yardley families had been among the first to leave England for William Penn's new colony. Fifty years later the grandchildren of those Quaker immigrants were themselves ready to move on, enticed by reports of fertile land newly open to settlement in Virginia. In the early 1730s Amos bought 400 acres on the south fork of Catoctin Creek from John Mead, who had obtained the land in a round-about way from Lord Fairfax, colonial proprietor of most of northern Virginia.[i]

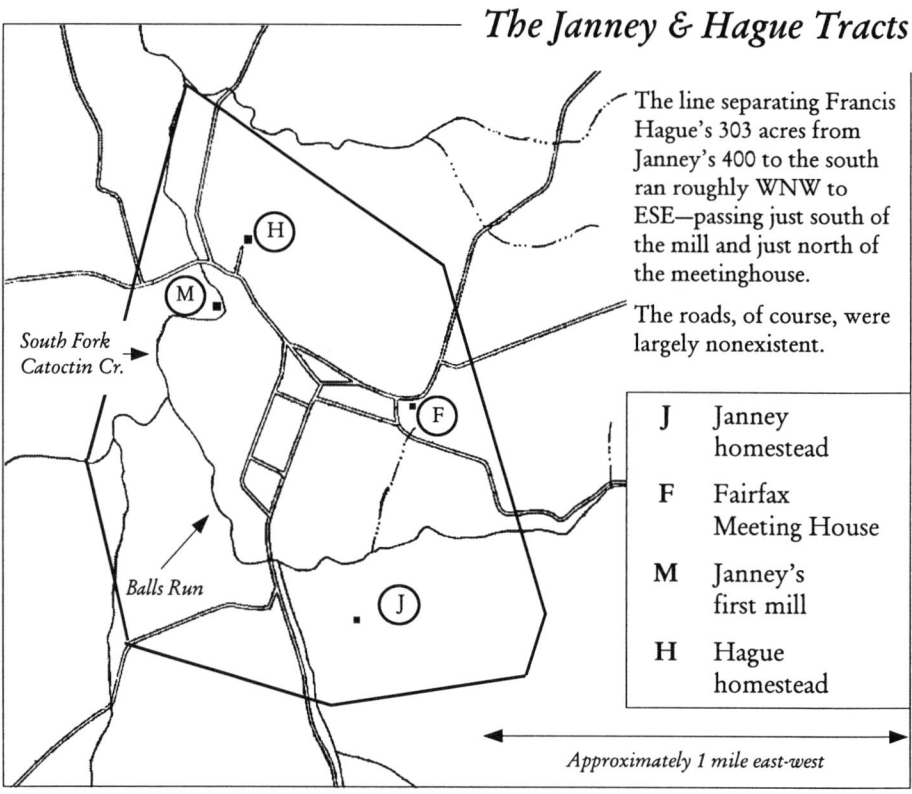

The Janney & Hague Tracts

The line separating Francis Hague's 303 acres from Janney's 400 to the south ran roughly WNW to ESE—passing just south of the mill and just north of the meetinghouse.

The roads, of course, were largely nonexistent.

J	Janney homestead
F	Fairfax Meeting House
M	Janney's first mill
H	Hague homestead

Approximately 1 mile east-west

---

[i] Prince William County Deed Book "C," the book recording the date of transfer to Amos Janney from land agent Catesby Cocke, has been missing since the Civil War. Thus an exact date is not available. Waterford dates its founding to 1733, based on the land transfers of the 703 acres between and among land agents John Mead, Richard Averill and Catesby Cocke.

The new home must have suited the Janneys; they evidently encouraged friends and relatives to join them from Pennsylvania. Among the first to follow were Mary's sister Jane and brother-in-law Francis Hague. In 1743 Hague bought from the same John Mead 303 acres abutting Janney's land on the northeast. Francis settled his large family in a modest stone cottage on a hill above Catoctin Creek.

In succeeding years Quakers arrived in growing numbers, drawn like Amos Janney by the promise of good land. Still, the trek from the north was not for the faint of heart. Even a full generation after Amos's pioneering move, the passage was still difficult as this letter home makes clear.

To William Myers
   in Kingwood, Hunterdon County, West Jersey

Dear Brother:

I thought proper to let thee know that we are all in good health at present which we have reason to be thankful for. Hoping these lines may find thee and all our dear friends and relations so. I have nothing strange at this time to write. I thought it would be acceptable to thee to have some account of our journey which was really troublesome for we had a great deal of wet weather and exceedingly bad roads and high water which was a great hindrance to us in crossing the ferries.

The Seventh day of the Fifth Month we left Kingwood and the Seventeenth we crossed the Potomac River, twelve miles from our house.

I can not give any particular account of how we like the place till firther trial, but we find it near as we expected, and live among good neighbors which is a blessing to be esteemed.

So I shall conclude and we whose names are here subscribed do salute you all in true love. Desiring your welfare and that you may be established in truth and perfect peace which is above all things desirable, therefore we shall take our leave of you all at this time.

The 7th day of the 6th Month 1761   *Farewell*
                                                       Jonathan Myers
                                                       Mary Myers

Not everyone was as cautious as the travel-weary Myers in appraising the new neighborhood. In April 1776, Thomas Rankin, a young Methodist preacher, described his ride from Frederick, Maryland, through the Waterford area to Leesburg in terms that would make even a modern-day developer blush.

> *This was the most pleasant day's ride I have had this spring. It was indeed lovely beyond description in crossing that fine river, the Potomack. The natural flowers on the banks, the large trees hanging over the sides of the river, adorned the green of different shades; while the broad limpid stream glided gently along, joining its murmurs with the tuneful tribes who made the woods vocal with their creator's praise. Here nature sported her virgin fancies and wantoned as in her prime! I could have sat on the banks of this delightful river all the day with the utmost pleasure....*[3]

Even Rankin conceded, however, that there were a few problems in this eden. He reported that panthers were numerous in the Waterford area. A local land-owner, Captain William Douglass, presented him with the pelt of one. It *"...measured 11 feet; and allowing 4 feet and 1/2 for the length of the tail, the body of the animal was upwards of 6 feet long."*

Wolves too were plentiful and a real threat to settlers' livestock. In 1757 local authorities paid Joseph Janney (cousin of Amos)[i] 100 pounds of tobacco for a wolf's head—the standard bounty.[4]

---

[i] This Joseph Janney—and there were several—was probably the Joseph who married Hannah Jones in Pennsylvania in 1764. He was the son of Abel and Sarah Baker Janney and a great-grandson of Thomas, the original Janney immigrant from England. Joseph died about 1793.

FAIRFAX MEETING

As the Myers' letter home suggests, these early Quakers were a devout people, and they carried their God with them. So when Amos Janney and his family left settled Bucks County for the wilds of Virginia's Northern Neck, they wasted no time setting up a new church or meeting, to use the Quaker term. There being no meetinghouse within many miles of his homestead on Catoctin Creek, Amos worshipped first in his own house and in those of fellow Quakers who had joined him from Pennsylvania. By 1741 enough Friends—as they called themselves—had gathered in the Loudoun Valley to build a small meetinghouse of logs and to set aside space for a schoolhouse and cemetery. They called the place Fairfax Meeting after the county—Loudoun would not be organized from western Fairfax as a new county until 1757.

These Quakers maintained a strict discipline among themselves and—fortunately for us—kept detailed church records. They met twice a week, on Sunday or First Day, as they preferred to call it, and again in mid-week. I remember one old Quaker nearly two hundred years later downing his tools on Wednesdays when it was time for meeting.

The Religious Society of Friends, like the Puritans before them, had emerged from the political and spiritual turmoil of 17th-century England. They believed in plain living and shunned the ceremony and hierarchy of the established Anglican Church. Strictly egalitarian, they sought understanding through an "inner light" and therefore had no use for a formal clergy. Their meetings involved periods of meditation, punctuated by prayers and exhortations from those so moved.

Those not of the faith tended to view the Quakers as clannish and a bit peculiar. A visiting Englishman, Nicholas Cresswell, attended a service at Waterford in February 1776. He praised the accommodations but was dubious about the content.

"[It was] *one of the most comfortable places of Worship I was ever in, they had two large fires and a Dutch stove. After a long silence and many groans a Man got up and gave us a short Lecture with great deliberation. Dined at Mr. Joseph Janney's one of the Friends.*"[5]

Despite the hospitality young Cresswell was less favorably impressed on his next visit, in October. *"Mr. Booker and I went to the Quaker Meeting, but were too late, tho' it would have been equally as well as if we had been sooner, for the spirit did not move any of them to speak. Can't conceive what service the people can receive by grunting and groaning for two or three hours without speaking a word. This is a stupid religion indeed."* He might have been more charitable if he had not been coming off an evening in Leesburg a few days earlier in which—by his own rueful account—he had got *"most feloniously drunk."*[6]

In any event, the meetinghouse Cresswell had admired in February 1776 was not the simple log structure of 1741. The Friends had erected a more substantial stone building in 1761, and in 1771 they doubled its size. Clearly the Quaker settlement was growing rapidly, the result of new immigrants from the north and large, healthy families. Amos Janney's brother-in-law Francis Hague, for example, sired at least twelve children—some descendants count 14 or more!

With all those children, it was probably inevitable that some would be less surely guided by the "inner light" than Francis, a founding member of Fairfax Meeting. The Meeting disowned Francis, Jr., in 1780 for "joining the Revolutionary Army." They took him back that same year, though, when he "confessed himself" shortly before his death.

Daughter Mary also strayed. At age 18 she was asking the meeting's forgiveness for her "fornication." Contrition did not bring abstinence. Two and a half years later, in 1757, churchwardens of the dominant Anglican Church hauled her up on charges of having a "base born child." John Ball finally made an honest woman of her; they married in 1761.[7]

Now I am not passing judgment on Ms. Hague's conduct. After all, I discovered late in my explorations of Waterford's past that my own great-grandmother bore two children—twins—without benefit of clergy. Sometimes it does not pay to dig too deep!

FAIRFAX MEETING HOUSE as enlarged in 1771.

JANNEY'S MILL

The newcomers had come to the Loudoun Valley in search of fertile land; most of them were farmers first. But as the little community grew there was need and opportunity for other skills and services. In the 1730s and 40s, for instance, Amos Janney made a name for himself in the Northern Neck as a surveyor. And since the settlers' chief crops were grain, he also saw a profit to be made as a miller.

With his surveyor's eye, Janney surely had in mind the power potential of the South Fork of Catoctin Creek and its tributary Balls Run when he bought his original 400 acres. We know that he soon built a simple mill of logs to harness that power. That mill is said to have been across the creek from and a hundred or so feet upstream of the mill we know today. It not only ground grain but sawed logs into beams and planks. Curiously, Janney built on Francis Hague's property—there must have been a strong handshake between the two Quaker relatives to bind that bargain.

Amos Janney died just a few years later in 1747—whether from disease or accident we do not know; he was only 45 or so. Fortunately his only surviving son, 16-year-old Mahlon, inherited his father's energy and acumen.[i]

Mahlon eventually erected a larger, two-story mill "of wood and of stone"[8] on a near-by site, which he eventually bought from his Uncle Francis in 1762 "with improvements thereon."[9] For more than half a century after the family's arrival the tiny settlement that developed around the structure was known simply as Janney's Mill. Over the years many other mills were built in the area, but the one Waterford now calls simply "the mill" remained the best known.

Mahlon Janney leased and then sold his mill to Jonas Potts several years before he died in 1812; ownership changed hands many times after that.[ii] It was apparently Thomas Phillips who around 1831 rebuilt Mahlon's mill into the three-story brick structure that stands today.

THE MILL AND ITS RACE as it appeared early in the 20th century. The additions at the rear of the building have since been removed.

---

[i] There have been many Mahlons in Waterford's long history. This Mahlon (pronounced MAY-lun) was born in 1731 or 1732; he died in 1812.
[ii] See page 22 for a list of owners of the mill.

No matter who the mill owner, there was always interesting activity in that end of town. In my time, "Parks and Recreation" was a phrase unheard of, so each youngster made his or her entertainment with what was at hand. Quite often it revolved around the mill. The large wheat and shelled-corn bins offered fun when we could jump from a height of several feet to sink into the grain. This could be done only if we managed to sneak by the miller to the upper floors where the bins were. I got one of the better beatings of my life one day when I got caught in the bin and then didn't get out quick enough when the miller's assistant told me to leave. Then there was the cob bin, which offered hiding places and ample ammunition for corn cob wars.

There was another use for the corn cobs, incidentally. Sarah Rucker Gordon (1896-1992) remembered it was one of her family jobs as a child to go to the mill around suppertime, especially in the summer when there might not be a good bank of coals in the cookstove, and buy—for five cents—a large sack of dry cobs for a quick fire start in the stove or to increase the speed of one.

Teams of four or six horses would haul in wheat or corn to be ground into flour or meal. I even saw a yoke of oxen come to the mill one day, the only ones I ever saw in Waterford. Henry Clapham, a farmer from near Milltown[i] north of the village, had this team, and it was a sight to see those two oxen go swinging along.

In my youth a metal-clad frame elevator was attached to the west or creek end of the mill. This also housed a cider mill in the early to mid-1920s where the men pressed cider one day a week in the fall months. A row of horse stables stood about forty feet behind the elevator. In my time, I can remember the miller owned only one four-horse team. But a historian writing of Civil War days recorded that Samuel C. Means,[ii] the prosperous miller of that time, had 28 horses at the outbreak of war to haul his products across the Potomac to Point of Rocks for shipment on the B&O Railroad or C&O Canal, and for other mill-related hauling.[10]

---

[i] Some historians occasionally refer to "Milltown" as an early name of the village that is now Waterford. I have seen no evidence to persuade me of that. There is, however, a tiny settlement called Milltown about two miles north of Waterford (at the intersection of modern Rts. 681 & 692).
[ii] Samuel Carrington Means (1827-1884). More about Sam Means later.

Left:
MILLER above steel wheel that replaced the old wooden mill wheel.

Below:
WHITE LILY FLOUR is the brand I most associate with the mill, but in its final years in operation the owners adopted the Quakertown label.

Owners of the Mill

Amos Janney	c.1741-1747
Mahlon Janney	c.1752-1808
Jonas Potts	1808-1814
Emanuel Newcomer	1814-1817
Jozabed White & Robert Braden	1817-
Robert Braden	-1826
Thomas Phillips (3 generations)	c.1831-
S. McPherson/E. Bond	
Nathan Walker	1848-1859
Samuel C. Means	1859-1868
Oliver Lantz	1868-1883
Chas. R. Paxson	1883-1889
A.S. Bates	1889-
W.M. Fling	-1916
V.E. Mays	1916-1922
W.S. Smoot	1922-
Waterford Mills, Inc.	
Waterford Foundation	1944-

ANNOUNCEMENT

Waterford Mills, Inc.

Established 1740

Have the Pleasure of
INTRODUCING

QUAKERTOWN

CORN MEAL, (White and Yellow) Made By
The Famous Method of Water Grinding
On The BURRSTONE

QUAKERTOWN

WHITE FLOUR, ELECTRICALLY BLEACHED

QUAKERTOWN

WHOLE WHEAT FLOUR---BUCKWHEAT FLOUR

Waterford, Va.

Phone Waterford 12-F-12   A. S. White, Manager
W. O. Tinsman, Miller

The millrace was quite an engineering feat for its 18th-century builders, both in design and construction in diverting water to drive the mill. A dam across the main body of Catoctin Creek started water on its way toward the mill carried by nearly a mile of race.

On its course, it picked up waters of Balls Run through a curious contraption called The Chute. This had overhead bridging supporting swinging gates that turned the water of the run at the race junction but also allowed flood waters to push open the swinging gates. Two small lift gates, one between the dam and the chute, and one between the chute and the mill, were used to flush the race of silt. I can remember some nights during a summer thunderstorm seeing the miller or his helper, with lantern in hand, going up the race to lift the gates to release the flood, his lantern bobbing as he rushed to get to each gate.

In the mill's later years a gasoline or kerosene engine was added for power so that grinding would not be interrupted in times of drought. The old overshot waterwheel and later turbine were giving way to a more modern way of milling. But the noisy exhaust from the engine never matched the distinctive rhythmic rumble of the big wheel. The romance of water-driven mills was gone and with it waterground meal and Waterford's White Lily flour, that being the trade name of the product that came from the mill.

The old mill finally gave way to modern production and merchandising, and its turning wheel halted forever during the Great Depression. Since 1943-44 the handsome old building has taken on a new role housing crafts during the Waterford Foundation's annual Fair.

Just across Main Street from the mill—near a shed that still stands—was a set of heavy-duty scales. They may once have been an adjunct to the mill, but I cannot recall grain being weighed there. Wagonloads of hay and straw were weighed from time to time, but cattle furnished the principal business for the scales—this was the transfer point from seller to buyer. Holding pens stood on the northeast side of the building. After weighing and settlement, the cattle were usually driven to the Washington & Old Dominion station at Paeonian Springs but occasionally to other points.[i]

---

[i] The hamlet of Paeonian Springs lies some three miles from Waterford and a mile west of Clark's Gap. It was founded in 1892, 22 years after the railroad had been

Six-horse team and wagon at the scales

As a youngster I helped drive cattle for stock dealer E. H. Beans from the railroad at Paeonian Springs to Waterford. These cattle were resold to farmers who would fatten them for slaughter, then sell to a dealer or a buyer for a packing house.

Mr. Beans had a border collie, Laddie, who was equal to two or three boys in handling cattle on the road. Laddie knew every side road or open gate between Waterford and the railroad. He would get ahead of the herd and be standing at the opening when the cattle got there. Once the drive passed this trouble spot, he would take off across the fields and be waiting when the first steer reached the next such temptation. He was a valuable little dog.

---

extended west beyond Leesburg. Before 1870, Point of Rocks, Maryland, had been the railroad station nearest Waterford. Village ledgers record much commerce through this town in the 1850s.

But I have gotten ahead of myself. If we could return to Janney's Mill as the American colonies neared revolution, we would find the place still just a small settlement. Along the boundary between Janney's and Hague's land, a blacksmith shop and tannery were apparently operating in addition to the mill. These three industries would have been essential to the growing agrarian economy.

We do not know much about the blacksmith shop, but the area just south of the scales across Liggett Street was used for many years as a tanyard. A 1785 deed description mentions as the Tanyard Branch a little spring-fed stream that crosses Main Street about a hundred yards south of the mill. From this we may assume that a tanyard was in existence before that date.

There were actually two tanneries in the general area—they may have overlapped for a time. The upper tanyard was owned first by William Hough (1744-1815) and son Joseph (1770-1806), and later by Joseph Bond.

The Houghs' operation was more modest than the one just downstream that followed; Thomas Phillips (c.1783-1842) and Asa Moore Bond (c.1804-1878), brother of Joseph, owned the later enterprise as partners. One local resident remembered it as a *"great tannery full of tan bark and mysterious vats that looked black and terrible"* to her as a child.[i]

The vats were a series of pits in the ground where the hides were soaked first in a caustic lime solution to loosen the hair, fur or wool then in a strong brew of oak or other bark to tan or preserve them. A building stood there partially covering the vats.[ii] Those pits are still visible today beside the Tanyard Branch in what we now call the Bond Street meadow.

Archeologist Dan Kent and his students from Loudoun County High School recently made a great contribution to Waterford history when they discovered the remains of a sizable building on the south side of the branch that apparently was part of Bond's operation. We moderns do not remember a house ever standing there, but early maps show one, and the real evidence is now at hand after so many years of being hidden

---

[i] Mary Chamberlin, who married William Clendenin.
[ii] The foundation of this building appears on aerial infrared photography of the area taken in April 1996.

by the earth.[i] While referred to in the deeds as a storehouse, it appears to have been a dwelling for a tanyard worker at at least one point in its history. More research needs to be done on this.

By the way, on a snowy day, with the sun at just the right angle, a practiced eye can also detect in the meadow the shadowy remnant of a hand-dug well that no doubt played some part in the tannery operation. In my father's youth, a horse standing in that meadow put a hoof through the turf, to everyone's astonishment, and they realized an old well had been abandoned and rather poorly blocked over with then-rotting timbers. They filled it in.

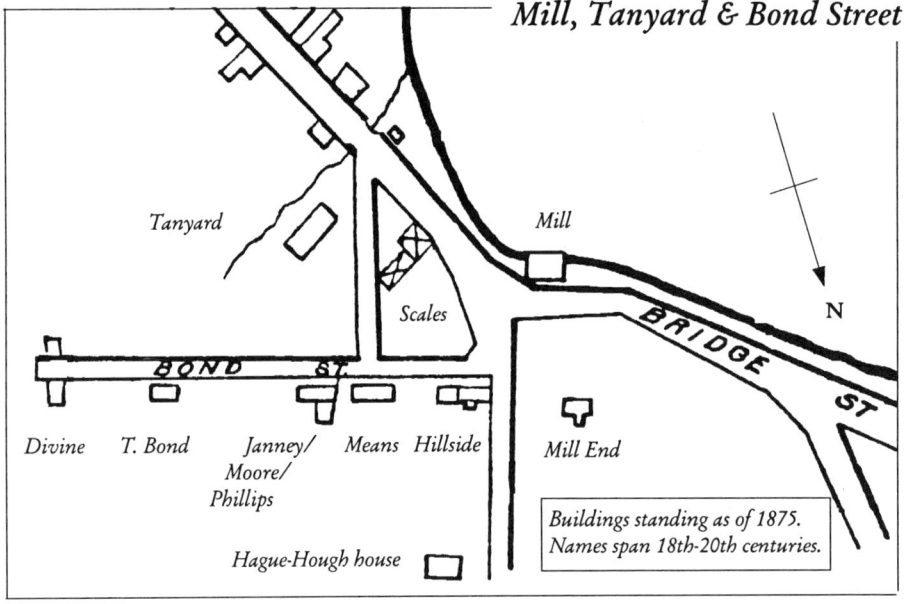

Mill, Tanyard & Bond Street

Buildings standing as of 1875. Names span 18th-20th centuries.

---

[i] The research, conducted over the summers of 1994 and 1995, revealed a structure roughly 20 x 24 feet with two brick chimneys. The building appeared to have been built of wood with a stone foundation in the late 18th or early 19th century. Artifacts found include many household items.

Wells—and Ills

These old hand-dug wells were a common and necessary feature of Waterford homes and businesses but they were real hazards too. One November day in 1819 Stephen Ball stopped by James Moore's place on Main Street Hill before heading home at the end of the day. In the dark of that autumn evening, he "by some unfortunate accident" fell into Moore's well, fractured his skull and died. An inquest determined that the deceased had been "neither intoxicated nor in any manner deranged."

The same could not be said for poor Israel Griffith some 20 years later. Griffith lived on Main Street and as secretary of the town council was a respected member of the community. But late one night in September 1839, in an unexplained fit of despair, he threw himself down his well and drowned.

The greatest problem with those old wells was contamination. They played a sinister role in epidemics of "bilious fever" [typhoid] and other plagues that regularly ravaged Waterford families. One of the worst outbreaks of typhoid began in 1821 with the arrival of warm weather, as was usually the case. In July, Obediah Cooksey lost three sons in two days. The next month my great-great-grandfather William Wright succumbed, then his wife Jane and son William. By October, David and Elizabeth Janney had died, leaving six small children. Many others perished, including the young, the old, and even visitors from out of town.

But to return to the settling of the land along Catoctin Creek in the 1700s, we find that the Janneys and Hagues were soon followed by other Quaker families: Taylors from Falls Monthly Meeting in Bucks County, Browns, Williams (1760s), and Moores (1780s) from Gwynedd and Uwchlan Meetings—all in Pennsylvania; Bonds and Walkers from the same colony via Hopewell Meeting in Winchester, Virginia. The Houghs and Steers had also arrived by 1765. All would play leading roles over many years in the development of Waterford.

In the 1760s the early Quakers were joined by numbers of Presbyterians, Methodists, Lutherans and Baptists. This influx of non-Anglicans is noteworthy considering the firm hold of the established Church of England in colonial Virginia. One enabling factor was the Toleration Act of the late 1600s that permitted dissenting congregations to live in Virginia, although all were obliged to pay an irksome tithe (*i.e.*, poll tax) on each male older than 16 years for support of the Anglican Church.[i] In practice, another factor may have been more important for those who would settle in Cameron Parish (present day Loudoun County). The parish minister appointed in 1749, one John Andrews, was said to have been constantly in debt, with alcohol his constant companion, and unable to police his parish. He was separated from the ministry in 1768, but by then non-Anglicans were firmly established around Waterford and elsewhere.

The local Presbyterian community, for example, had apparently begun to worship together by 1764 led by Amos Thompson, a recently ordained minister from the College of New Jersey—later Princeton University. Many in his congregation had come, as had the Quakers, from eastern Pennsylvania and New Jersey. In 1769 John Micklehaney [McIlhaney], Jenkins David, William Douglass (he of the panther skin), Flemming Patterson, Peter Ker [Carr], Nathaniel Patterson and William Cavins bought for their church near Janney's settlement "one acre of ground with the house erected thereon."[ii]

Whether Scotch-Irish immigrants or Pennsylvania Quakers, most of the new-comers lived well outside Janney's Mill. On the site of the future village itself, few lots were available for building because Francis Hague and Mahlon Janney still owned most of the land.

That situation finally changed in 1780 when Hague died. His will directed that his lands be sold, wholly or separately, and the following year his son and executor Thomas sold 12 acres to Joseph Janney.[11] In short order, lots were marked off on the north side of Main Street, and in 1791 Janney laid out 15 more along the south side, from the Mill almost to the existing Post Office—divisions that are clear to this day.

---

[i] Francis Hague attempted his own tax revolt against this levy in 1753 but was soon brought into line. [See endnote 6.]

[ii] The church was built on the Clark's Gap road just south of what is now the intersection of Rts. 662 and 703.

In 1800, Mahlon Janney, continuing the momentum, began selling lots on the extension of Main Street up the "Big Hill," and in 1812 when he died, his executors subdivided his land along Second and High Streets.

By the turn of the century then, nearly 70 years after Amos Janney's arrival, the little settlement was beginning to take on the appearance of a real town. Readers at this point might be interested in some of the particular places and people that have shaped it.

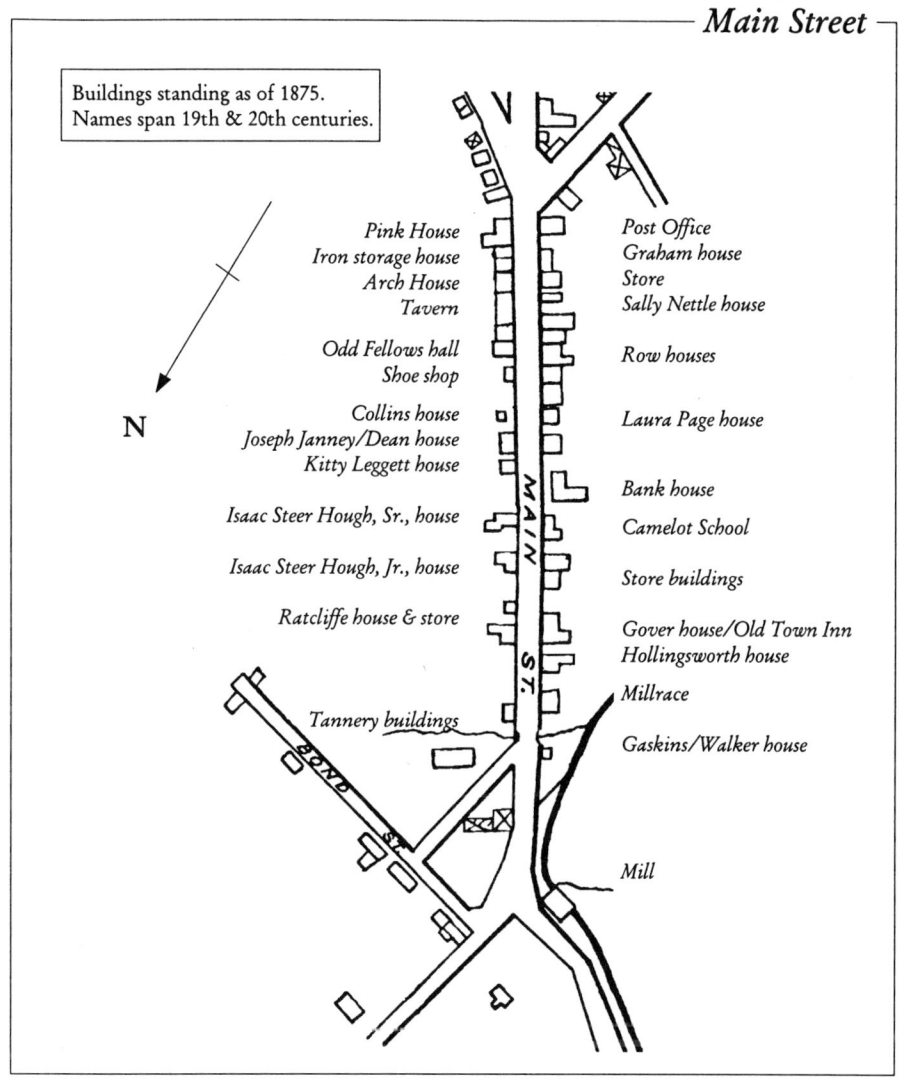

Personal Estate of Francis Hague[12]

The things a man leaves behind provide insight into his life and times. These few animals, simple tools, and utilitarian furnishings are the material legacy of one of Waterford's founders and leading citizens.

Sundry wearing apparel	Two Saddles	1 Stack Hay
1 Riding mare Saddle & Bridle	1 broken Iron Pott	1 Hogshead
1 Bed Bedstead & furniture	1 pair Iron Tongs	Sundry Horse gears
1 Bedstead of furniture	1 Bake Iron	1 Ox Chain
1 Warming Pan	1 old Shovel	2 Bells
1 Woman's saddle	2 Pott Racks	Rings & Wedges
1 Old Desk	1 Wheel/2 pr. Cards	1 Tea Kettle
4 Old Tubs	1 Iron Skillit	1 Steer
1 Old Chest	1 Frying Pan	1 Heifer
1 Armed Chair	1 Sow and 8 Piggs	1 Brindle Cow
Small bundle toe [tow]	6 large Hogs	2 Spring Calfs
21 Large Spools	18 Head Sheep	1 Red Steer
1 Pr Scales and Weights	1 Bay Colt	1 Brindle Steer
1 Hone & Whetstone	1 Grey Horse	1 Swarm Bees, 3 Bee Gums
1 Side soal [sic] leather	1 Iron Kettle	1 Cross Cut Saw
1 Calf Skin	2 Old Scythes	2 Baggs
1 Pair Upper Leather	1 Old Bedstead	1 Fox Trap
1 Razor	1 Old Tubb	Old gears
1 pr. Stillyards [steelyards]	1 Dough Trough	2 Pitch Forks & Rakes
1 Flax Heckle [hackle]	1 Bowl	2 Broad Hoes
1 Old Box Iron	1 Pair Hand [sic] Irons	2 Barrells
1 Brass Heckle	1 Crow Bar	2 Old Hogshead
2 Pair Sheep Shears	3 Axes	1 Ghegg
1 Lanthorn [sic]	1 Piece of Steel	Sundry Old Tubbs
1 Looking Glass	1 Pr. Hinges & Hammer	1 Brass Cock
1 Smooth bore Gun	3 Augurs	1 Raw Hide
7 Old Chairs	Sundry Old Iron	1 Old Hogshead
4 Old Water Pails	1 Pr. Candlemoulds	Broke Hemp
2 Tables	1 Plough Clevices	Cart Iron
1 Sieve	2 Collars & Swingletree	1 Cutting Box & Knife
1 Hair Sifter	1 Plow & Ditto	1 Half Bushel
Sundry Books	1 Iron Tooth'd Harrow	1 Mattock
Sundry Pewter	1 Old Barrel	1 Still & Worm
Old Earthen Ware	1 Old Waggon	1 Dutch Fan
4 Tin Cups	2 Rye Stacks	1 Mow Hay
5 Trenchers	2 Iron Spaids	1 Brindle Cow
11 Still Tubs	1 Pewter Funnel	2 Tubbs
4 Gheggs [sic]	1 Hoe & Harrow	3 Pails 1 Tub

The oldest structure remaining in the village is probably Francis Hague's little stone cottage above the mill to the north. William Hough bought the remainder of Hague's Waterford holdings in 1788 and soon after he greatly enlarged the house with an imposing brick addition, making it then and now one of the finest homes in Waterford.

This is the same William Hough who owned the upper tanyard—and a lot more besides.[i] His father, "Old John" Hough, by 1765 held some 5,000 acres, more than anyone else actually resident in the county. The Houghs, like their cousin Amos Janney, were surveyors and businessmen in addition to farmers, and canny enough to capitalize on every opportunity in growing Loudoun County.[13]

Between the Hague-Hough house and the mill is another handsome federal-style brick residence, *Mill End*. Traditionally the home of the miller, this house was built shortly after 1814 by Emanuel Newcomer, who owned the mill at the time.

MILL END

The porch was not original to the building and has since been removed. Similar additions have come and gone on many houses in Waterford as need and fashion have changed.

---

[i] William Hough (1744-1815). William's father John (1719/20-1797) had come to Loudoun from Pennsylvania before 1750.

One of my earliest village memories is of *Mill End*'s two elderly occupants, Mrs. Jake Walker and Mrs. Mary Ruth Williams.[i] These ladies, sisters-in-law, were a bridge to Waterford's past. Mrs. Walker was the widow of Quaker Jacob Walker, Waterford's postmaster from 1897 to 1907. Her father-in-law, Nathan Walker, had owned the mill at one point and been president of the Loudoun Mutual Fire Insurance Company.[ii] Mary Ruth Williams was Nathan's daughter but more particularly the second wife and widow of William Williams, the community's leading citizen during the Civil War. I am glad I can say that I remember these two gallant ladies as symbols of the past, both as members of the Society of Friends and survivors of the Civil War.

Across John Brown's Lane[iii] from *Mill End* is Bond (originally Back) Street, a single block that includes some of the earliest houses in Waterford. Anchoring the west end of Bond Street is an old clapboard-covered house we now call *Hillside*. It did not have a name until more recent times. During my early youth it was owned by Uncle Tom Mallory and his good wife Henrietta. "Ret" was large, very black, and the greatest friend a little boy ever had, a wonderful cook whose kitchen emitted aromas that said "a new batch of cookies is in the making, come and get them." A part of this house was the first post office in the town (established on November 20, 1800), but that bit of history was secondary to a little boy more interested in cookies.

White children, by the way, called black adult good friends "aunt" or "uncle." The black children would refer to most elders of their own race in the same way but used "Mr.," "Mrs.," or "Miss" in referring to white and highly esteemed black adults. According to Sarah Gordon, an African-American born in Waterford in 1896, the same rule generally applied to black children addressing white children.

---

[i] Mary Gilkesan Walker (1841-1930) & Mary Ruth Walker Williams (1838-1926).

[ii] The Loudoun Mutual Fire Insurance Company was founded in Waterford in 1849 with 13 directors, Nathan Walker among them; the company remains today a thriving business, Waterford's largest.

[iii] This name was given in error by a former resident. It does not refer to the abolitionist John Brown, who led the 1859 raid on the federal arsenal at nearby Harpers Ferry, but to *Joseph* Brown (1821-1893), who owned the Hague-Hough house for some years.

"If they were poor like us, we called 'em by their first name; otherwise, we had to call 'em 'Miss' or 'Mr.' with their first names." I was poor so I did not know this at the time, but Sarah Gordon was an astute person.

I remember Uncle Tom Mallory lived by the almanac that furnished the signs for his planting. According to him, if the seed was not planted in the right sign, you might just as well throw it away. One year he pushed back snow to get a few hills of potatoes in the ground on St. Patrick's Day. Uncle Tom was also a very hard worker. I remember one time he dug a well in his front yard. After thirty feet, it was apparent that it was a dry hole. Uncle Tom filled it back in.

Abutting *Hillside* on the east until about 1920 was a still older fieldstone structure built in Mahlon Janney's time as a miller's house. It was later used for mill storage, then reverted once more to a dwelling until it was finally torn down to make more space for a chicken yard. It is tragic that this house was demolished for, if standing today, it would be the third oldest house in the Waterford area. Only Amos Janney's portion of the house at Talbott Farm, just outside the village, and Francis Hague's end of the Hague-Hough house were built earlier.

Hillside and mill storage building

Aunt Jennie Boyd lived in that now-vanished building. She was the first corpse that I ever saw—I must have been six or seven at the time. She cooked the evening meal for the Ernest James family, two doors down, and died sitting in a chair in their kitchen. A scene never to be forgotten was peeping in the window to see what all the excitement was about and seeing Aunt Jennie propped in that chair.

> Of course death was a closer companion in old Waterford than in these days of hospitals, antibiotics, and nursing homes. Sometimes very close. Gladys Lewis tells of her young sisters sharing a bed in the 1920s, as was common in those days. One of them, on waking up and finding her sister had crowded her to the edge of the bed, gave her a kick to rouse her and get her back on her side. To her shock, the sister was "stone cold," having died in the night. The cause was an undiagnosed case of typhoid.
>
> Not every passing was so jolting. One very young girl in the village, when asked how her ailing grandfather was getting along, replied, *"Just the same as yesterday, only he is dead."*

Possibly no place in Waterford has been home to as many persons in the news as the next house to the east on Bond Street, a stone and brick structure that villagers variously call the Mahlon Janney/Asa Moore/Sam Means house. Mahlon Janney built the stone portion about 1762 as his mill operations flourished. A later resident, Asa Moore (c.1770-1823), was an engineer who left many scientific books in his collection at his death. He had participated in canal operations in Ohio, but his greatest works were in the Waterford area, developing both land and the fulling mills.[i]

---

[i] "Fulling" is an old process used to increase the weight and bulk of cloth, especially wool, by controlled shrinking and beating.

Still later, at the time of the Civil War, the miller Sam Means owned the house. He was a lapsed Quaker, according to lore,[14] and an interesting character. An avowed supporter of the Union, Means received a direct commission from Secretary of War Stanton early in the conflict to raise a company for the army. (His Quaker wife Rachel was greatly distressed by his decision to fight.) This company became the Loudoun Rangers, the only such organized unit from what is now Virginia to fight for the Union. Stories connected with this house and with Sam Means are too numerous to tell here.

Just to the east of Mahlon Janney's house on Bond Street, his cousin Joseph Janney bought land and built a small log house around 1780. Not long after, Joseph sold the property to Thomas Moore, a Pennsylvania Quaker who arrived in October of that year. Moore brought with him his wife Elizabeth and three children, one of them the Asa just mentioned; older sons James and Thomas, Jr., also moved to the area in 1780.[15]

Local tradition has long had it that the elder Moore had the village renamed for his native Waterford in Ireland, and it is true that at *about* the time that he arrived Janney's Mill began to be called Waterford. But Moore came to Waterford from Uwchlan Monthly Meeting in Pennsylvania, and I have seen no evidence that he was born in Ireland, so I don't regard the tradition as proved.

Later owners of the property include Quakers Thomas Phillips and Asa Bond. Bond also lived for a time in the small two-story brick house next door. This dwelling may have been built by Asa Moore, but afterward for many years it was the home of the prominent Bond family.

Asa Moore's sister Elizabeth married Joseph Bond on New Years Eve, 1794, and their children—Joseph Jr., Ann, Thomas, Asa and Edward Bond—were to play a major role in the history of the village.[16] Joseph Bond, Jr., who owned and operated the upper tanyard after the Houghs, lived at one point in the small house with his brother Asa. Later it was the home of the third brother, Dr. Thomas Bond, the "Healer of Waterford" during the terrible years of war that struck the town. The fourth brother, Edward, owned the mill from 1832 to 1848; he was also Waterford's second mayor. No wonder they renamed this block Bond Street.

I remember two additional houses on the east end of Bond Street that are no longer standing. One was a brick structure that stood on the north side of the street. It was built by Edward Stabler,[i] quite possibly in the early days of the 19th century. This house may have been a two-story building like its neighbor to the west, but in my lifetime it was crumbling. Directly across the street there was a clapboard-sheathed log house, built by my great-great-grandfather Jacob Divine[ii] in 1816. This log house was last occupied—until about 1920—by a black man, Jim Simms.

There was one more building on Bond Street, at the corner with Liggett Street. I mention it last because it was built much later (1891) than the others. This is the John Wesley Methodist Episcopal Church, in my time a central building in the black community. Religious services, Children's Day, and funerals drew large crowds and brought forth the greatest music. I am sure the Good Lord had a special place for Annie Ferrell and her beautiful voice in His Angel Choir when He called her home. Time has not erased the memory of her spine-tingling singing at all important occasions.

All churches need their dedicated members if they are to survive and become important to the community. At the risk of omitting several just as qualified or as dedicated, I'd like to recall two who made many contributions to the life of John Wesley. One was Edward Gaskins, a long-time superintendent of the Sunday School. Ed not only was active in the church but—more impressive to a boy like me at the time—he had powers to remove warts and sties, a practice called "pow-wowing." This is probably a lost art these days since dermatologists have come around.

Ed Gaskins, was born about 1863, the son of Moses Gaskins and grandson of Judy Gaskins, both of whom had been freed by one William Tate in Loudoun County in 1849.[17] The black community of Waterford always called him Dr. Gaskins. They believed that, because of his knowledge of folk medicine, his tall thin physique and very dark color, he had come directly from Africa, though as the record shows, he was

---

[i] Stabler, a prominent Alexandria Quaker with strong Waterford ties, had a daughter Elizabeth, who married Waterford's Joseph Bond, son of Joseph and Elizabeth Moore, Jr., in 1828. Waterford is deeply indebted to the late William Wade Hinshaw, Quaker chronicler *extraordinaire*, [see endnotes] for helping to sort out all these Edwards, Asas, Josephs and Elizabeths!
[ii] Jacob Divine (1784-1863).

born in Loudoun County. In some circles Ed was also credited with having special powers. Some claimed to have seen "his walking stick move like a snake."[i] He lived in the little log house on Main Street nearest the mill.

Another pillar of the church was George Washington Dean,[ii] ever the watchful eye of the congregation. A story has been told of Deacon Dean's stewardship. A new preacher had arrived to lead the flock and immediately started on a campaign to raise money, even to the extent of passing the collection plate a second time if he thought the contributors were lagging. All went well until this preacher's sermon on the theme that "Religion Is Free."

JOHN WESLEY CHURCH congregation, 1910
Deacon Dean is second from the left; Ed Gaskins is at far right.

---

[i] I must thank Gladys Jackson Lewis, who overheard adult conversations as a child, for reminding me of these bits of Waterford lore.
[ii] G.W. Dean lived with his wife, the former Mary Elizabeth Cleggett, in the Joseph Janney house on Main Street. George and Mary's grandson, Adolphus Fuller Dean, visited Waterford in 1992 and shared a great deal of family information, including information about the long straight black hair of his great-grandmother, Caroline/Clementine Cleggett—the record is inconsistent on the name—giving some credence to the family tradition that she was "the daughter of an Indian chief."

This was too much for Deacon Dean, so at the close of service he asked the preacher to explain, if religion was free, how come he passed the collection plate a couple of times and was always asking for money? The reply: "Brother Dean, I am glad you asked that question. Do you see that spring on the hillside with water gushing forth? That water is free, but you must pay to have it piped in."

End of explanation.

This might be a good place to digress a little on the broader history of Waterford's black community, which has been such an important part of the village for many generations.

From early days the unusual thing about Waterford was the number of free black people who lived in and around this southern town. Freed slaves were already living in the area in 1810, the date of the earliest surviving census. And at least one man, William Lane, was born free about 1795. For more than 100 years his descendants owned what has come to be called the *Weavers Cottage*.

The Quakers had long frowned on slavery and in 1776 banned it officially for Friends. Their egalitarian beliefs meant that former slaves found a haven in that small corner of Virginia.

This is not to say that Waterford for African Americans was a promised land, especially for those who were not free. Even a few Quakers kept slaves, to the distress of fellow Friends. Henry Taylor was one such sinner. He was "much laboured with" by delegations of Friends from 1762 until 1778 when finally he "condemned his former conduct in dealing with slaves." In 1785 there was a "complaint against Jane Connard for consenting to the buying of a slave."[18] And as late as 1841 Fairfax Meeting was obliged to disown Mary Hough for "owning slaves which she refuses to give up."[19]

Non-Quakers in the village had little such difficulty from their churches. Furniture maker John Mount, for instance, had one or two slave members of his household on Main Street as of 1840. And on farms out of town larger numbers of slaves were common: Sanford Ramey, at *Rosemont* west of Waterford, owned 19 as of 1788; east of town at about that time Joseph McGeach and Joseph Caldwell each had five or six slaves.

The circumstances of servitude were as varied as the slaves and owners themselves. In 1861 one of Sanford Ramey's kin rented out "Helen" for $70 for the year to a woman in Leesburg. He stipulated that she agree to *"treat the negro woman in a humane manner and to furnish her with good and comfortable bedding and with the necessary clothing...her summer clothing to be not less than two good strong cotton frocks and capes, two good strong cotton aprons, two good strong cotton chemises and a pair of good strong shoes."* He specified proper winter clothing as well, *"including two pair of good strong home-knit woolen stockings and a pair good strong shoes (to be made in the County)."* I have often wondered if my Great-Uncle Charlie Divine, might have been the local cobbler who made her pair of "good strong shoes."

Occasionally, in the dry language of legal documents, there are some real stories. Jacob Mock, a farmer north of the village, specified in his 1831 will that *"My Negro boy Henson...."* was to be freed at age 26 and given ten dollars in cash and a good suit of woolen clothing. Mock took pains to ensure that his *"executors provide for him so he shall not fall into a state of slavery again by operation of the laws of the state in which we live."*

The three witnesses to Mock's will were all Quakers; perhaps they encouraged the old man's generosity. Or maybe there was even a family connection: census records indicate that Henson had at least some white ancestry. We may never unravel the whole story.

We do know that Henson fathered a child, also named Henson [Young], who was born into slavery on January 6, 1846. The mother was probably a slave of Mock's neighbor, William Russell, Sr. In 1864, late in the Civil War, young Henson—by then freed by Russell—made his way to Baltimore, Maryland, and enlisted in the 1st U.S. Colored Troops Infantry. He was one of several African Americans from Waterford who served with Union units.

Henson senior, meanwhile, had been working hard and become prosperous, probably as a teamster. After the war he filed a claim with the government for six horses valued at $1,120 that had been taken by Waterford cavalry officer Sam Means in 1862 for his Loudoun Rangers.

Henson junior inherited his father's way with horses. I remember him driving a fine team when I was a child. He died in 1930.

In at least one household in Waterford a free black man owned a slave. Nathan Minor, who owned a house and lots on Water Street, appears to have purchased his wife—there was a slave woman of his approximate age living with him in 1820. This arrangement may not be as odd as it sounds. I have heard that in some cases this practice was meant to ensure that the slave did not fall back under white ownership. By 1830, though, she evidently had attained her freedom. The Minor children prospered; some stayed in the area and others left. I knew several of their grandchildren in the village.

After the war, of course, black people in Waterford enjoyed a new status. Not surprisingly, that change took some getting used to—on both sides of the racial fence. In the summer of 1865, 15-year-old Marie Matthews[i] noted in her diary her exasperation that *"Our servant walked off this morning without any ceremony whatever. It does make me so indignant to think of the colored people being so impudent."* Not exactly the noble sentiments you might expect from a daughter of one of Waterford's leading Quaker families.

A couple of months later, however, young Marie took a more selfless view.

Sept 24th. Father, Auntie and Sister Edie went to meeting. Uncle Sam [Gover] returned with them. Auntie and I wishing to go to the colored school held in Waterford, the Capt [Simon Elliott Chamberlin] hitched up and took us. I had been very much prejudiced before going, but I divested myself of all that and became Oh! so much interested in them. I hope I can get a class [as a teacher] as I should like to so much. I think [it] is "bread cast upon the waters and in time it will return."[20]

In the early days of Waterford there were other kinds of servitude involving both whites and free blacks that were not always entirely voluntary. Mahlon Janney, for instance, had a "servant," Duncan McDonald, who ran away for 35 days in 1769. When McDonald reappeared Janney took him to court.[21] McDonald had probably been

---

[i] Mary (Marie) Ruth Matthews (1850-1867), daughter of Edward Y. & Sarah Gover Matthews.

legally bound to Janney to serve a number of years as an apprentice. This was a common practice at the time.

Often it was the Overseers of the Poor who made the formal arrangements. Usually they would bind an orphaned or other needy teenager—though sometimes a much younger child—to a local tradesman, merchant or farmer. The child would earn his keep with his labor and, by learning a trade, would eventually become self-supporting.

That was the goal; the reality did not always measure up. Sometimes the apprentice ran off, to the consternation of the man who depended on his help. And on occasion the master neglected or abused his charge. In theory, and at least sometimes in practice, that was grounds for breaking the contract.

NORTH END of the village, from 1882 sketch

THE DEVELOPMENT OF MAIN STREET

I have already mentioned as the home of Ed Gaskins the small log house that stands just south of the mill. It was moved to this site before 1875 from a farm—Old John Hough's *Corby Hall*, I have heard—north of town. In 1920 this cabin was occupied by Dan Walker and his wife Violet (Vi). It was said that Dan was born a slave. I have seen no evidence to support that claim, though he was old enough to have been.[i] He was a handyman around town but may principally be remembered as the deliveryman for the *Sunday Star*. The postal service brought in this Washington paper six days a week, but on Sundays Dan was the only source of delivery. He met the train at Paeonian Springs and did house-to-house delivery. His means of transportation was Old Bob hitched to a buggy.

Dan and Old Bob on the Big Hill

---

[i] According to the 1920 census, Dan, then 70, would have been about 13 at the time of the Emancipation Proclamation in 1863.

Bob, small in size but game in heart, was a faithful servant to Uncle Dan. Occasionally Dan rode Bob, and what a sight! Bob was a little mustang type, and Dan was a big man whose feet nearly dragged the ground when mounted on the horse. Dan died in a corn shock while shucking for Mr. Arthur Phillips.[i] An important part of the town passed on with Dan and Bob.

This house was a bystander in a violent episode of the Civil War. On October 20, 1861, the Confederates, in an effort to capture Sam Means (who had fled to Maryland unbeknownst to his would-be captors), posted a picket at the Tanyard Branch flowing beside this cabin. That night a shot rang out, and the sentry, William Grubb,[ii] dropped dead. In Waterford, everybody knew everything that happened, sometimes even before it occurred. But this is one event that has remained a mystery; no one has ever come up with a name for the assassin.

WALKER/GASKINS house

---

[i] Arthur Willis Phillips (1859-1925) was a descendent of the Thomas Phillips who rebuilt the present mill. The Phillips farm was just northwest of the village.
[ii] William Grubb was a member of the Loudoun Cavalry that had been organized in 1859 at the time of the John Brown raid. It later became Company K of the 6th Virginia Cavalry.

The next house toward the center of town on the south side of Main Street is a small brick cottage that appears to be very old. I do not know much of its history, but I can say a little more about its neighbor.

That two-story brick dwelling was occupied during the Civil War by Robert Isaac Hollingsworth, a school teacher and member of the Society of Friends.[i] He and prominent businessman William Williams, a fellow Quaker, were seized by the Confederates and marched off to Richmond's Castle Thunder Prison as hostages for Henry Ball of Temple Hall and Campbell Belt of Rock Hall—farms on what is now Route 15. These two were being held by the Union at Fort Delaware.

Robert Isaac had a bad habit of chewing tobacco, much to the annoyance of Williams, who wrote in his account of their confinement: *"I asked him to move his things as I did not fancy sleeping in a pool of tobacco juice."* But he also had his strong points. After the war he was an officer in the Loyal Citizens of Loudon [sic] County, a local committee formed to help rebuild the shattered society.

On May 6, 1865, less than a month after General Lee's surrender at Appomattox, the group met in Waterford for the purpose of "organizing the County." The venerable S.B.T. Caldwell of Wheatland was appointed chairman, and H.C. Brown and Robert I. Hollingsworth were elected secretaries. The group resolved that *"with no desire to avenge the injuries we may have suffered, and with an earnest wish to heal the wounds inflicted on our beloved State by the late unparalleled war, we desire that such a course may be pursued by our State and national authorities as shall insure peace and tranquility to all, with as little suffering to any as is consistent with a due regard to the principles of justice, and the future peace and welfare of our common country."*

---

[i] Robert Isaac Hollingsworth (1814-1871) was one of the Hollingsworths of Hopewell Monthly Meeting at Winchester, in the Shenandoah Valley. He was a son of Lewis and Abigail Parkins Hollingsworth. Robert married Rachel Stone of Waterford in 1847 and soon after moved to her village, where their five children were born.

The log house beside the Hollingsworth place was built around 1795 and occupied by the Gover family[i] for two generations. The Govers were leading merchants during one period, and they had a pair of frame store buildings that ran nearly the entire distance of the street frontage between their dwelling and the next property. During the Civil War, they as Quakers were considered enemies of the Confederacy and were preyed on by rebel raiding parties. At one point, Sam Gover filed a claim for $3,000 worth of merchandise carried off by the Confederates. Eventually, both Gover and his wife had to flee to Maryland. She wrote from there to Secretary of War Stanton asking for Union protection to return to Waterford and take care of their property.

The building also housed the post office during one period (1862-1882), and Sam Gover was both merchant and postmaster. Mr. Gover was known to lack energy, preferring to sit in his chair rather than to wait on postal patrons. He had a young assistant, Tom,[ii] who was quite often obliged to tend store and post office. One day a postal patron came in and asked a reclining Sam Gover if he had any mail. Gover replied, "*No, thee does not have any mail.*" The patron thanked him and departed, whereupon Mr. Gover asked, "*Tom, who was that?*"

Early in this century the property was owned by Edgar James and his wife Lizzie.[iii] Edgar too was a storekeeper, as well as a Justice of the Peace for Jefferson District for many years. He died in 1918, but Lizzie stayed on in the place, running a boarding house she called the Oldtown Inn. The Inn's amenities included a substantial stone structure at the rear of the property dubbed The Lodge as well as a goldfish pond and a swimming pool that was less than successful at holding water because the cement shell was badly cracked from the beginning.[22]

Mrs. James' cooking at any rate must have been good. The directors of the Loudoun Mutual Fire Insurance Company would often take lunch there after their monthly meeting.

---

[i] Jesse Gover (1791-1842), son of Samuel and Sarah Janney-Harris Gover, married the former Miriam G. Taylor (1791-1863) in Waterford in 1814. Memorials prepared by Fairfax Meeting for both Jesse and Miriam attest to their faithful and inspirational service with the meeting. Of their five children, Samuel (1824-1907) married first Margaret Parkins in 1859, then on her death he wed the former Temperance Matthews in 1869.
[ii] John Thomas McGavack (1856-1941).
[iii] Edgar Clayton James (1861-1918) & Annie Elizabeth Hough James (1861-1936).

Lizzie's daughter Carrie married Clarence Hopkins from Washington. He eventually tore down the two dilapidated frame buildings along the street that had been used both as store and residence. He added the "gramophone" that stands in the lawn today and enlarged a portion of the old millrace behind the lodge to facilitate canoeing.

Next to Gover's old property is another log house. Patrick McGavack bought the lot it stands on in 1802 and held it until his death in 1826. He probably built the house, although one-person ownership makes it difficult to place a date on the building's construction.

McGavack was a noted weaver who at one time kept seven looms running for his business, according to a great-granddaughter. The weavers stayed with the McGavack family as part of their household. This was probably at the McGavack's home place, now *Catalpa Grove*, on the Wheatland road a couple of miles west of town.

One of McGavack's weavers was always careful to secure his old trunk whenever the house was left unoccupied. He would lock the trunk, then lift the lid from the hinge side, which was no longer attached, and drop the key inside. To his amused friends he would explain, "*Well, who would ever try to break into a trunk from the back?*"

McGavack clearly prospered. In addition to 204 acres at *Catalpa Grove*, he eventually acquired 300 more in Culpeper County and several properties in Waterford, besides the lot and log house on Main Street. Patrick Street in "New Town"[i] is named for him. In my time Andrew McGavack, a great-great-grandson, lived on Patrick Street, and Lewis McGavack, another descendant, owned *Sunnyside* on Second Street.

But back to Patrick the patriarch. On his death, the court ordered the estate sold and divided five ways among his heirs. That otherwise equitable arrangement worked a great hardship on McGavack's slaves: One, Grace, went to an under-aged daughter Pleasant; Grace's teenage son, Hanson, went to Patrick, Jr.; another son, George, who was only 8 or 9, went to Tamar McGavack Graham and her husband. The orphaned children of Patrick's son James shared Grace's four-year-old daughter Mary, while one-year-old Abby Ann went to another son, William.

Patrick's remaining son, Israel, incidentally, came to a bad end. In July 1842, with "a hempen cord of the value of six cents," he hanged himself in his barn. The coroner's inquest concluded that he had been "seduced and moved by the instigation of the devil."[23]

---

[i] "New Town," a name given to the subdivided lots sold on the south end of town after the death of Mahlon Janney in 1812, continued well into this century as a description of the area.

In 1847 Patrick's heirs sold the house on Main Street to Hugh McNulty (1791-1851), a tailor born in Ireland. Much later, during World War II, the building was used for a year as a school by Edward M. Chamberlin, Jr., and his wife Kathryn, hence the name *Camelot School*, a term still in use, although the house has been a dwelling for many years now.

The next structure on the south side of Main Street, a fine brick building, has seen both residential and commercial use. It was Isaac Steer's (1757-1844) home early in the 19th century. During his ownership, around 1815, the Loudoun Company—to the best of my knowledge the first bank in Loudoun County—held meetings in the basement, giving the place its current name—the *Bank House*. The Loudoun Company enjoyed two years of successful operation, but the government required such banking institutions to give ten percent of their stock for internal improvement, and this the conservative directors would not do.[i] So the Commonwealth refused it a charter and ordered it closed.[24]

$10 NOTE issued by the short-lived Loudoun Company

---

[i] The directors were brothers James & Asa Moore, Robert Braden, John Williams, Abiel Jenners, George Janney, Samuel Clapham, John Hamilton, Joshua Osbourn, Cornelius Shawen, John Morgan, and Jacob Mendenhall.

In 1849, local farmers and businessmen established the Loudoun Mutual Fire Insurance Company, setting up shop in the same basement office. That venture fared better. It not only survived but became a giant in Virginia insurance circles.[i]

In my early youth Mr. John William McKinney lived in the house. He was at one time a successful harnessmaker, then a livestock dealer. Mr. KcKinney, known as "John Dick," bought one of the early autos to come to town. He used his former carriage house and stable, which stood along the bank of the millrace, to garage his new purchase. On his first attempt to pull his car into this garage he ran through the back, and the front wheels settled in the race. He was forced to get a farmer to pull it out with horses. He then had two very large posts planted in the rear of the building to keep him out of the water.

LAURA PAGE house and weatherboard row houses

---

[i] The Insurance Company was incorporated by an act of the General Assembly of Virginia on March 12, 1949. The first directors were Noble S. Braden, George D. Smith, Robert L. Wright, Nathan Walker, Robert J. White, Daniel G. Smith, Henry T. Gover, Sanford I. Ramey, Washington Vandevanter, Henry Russell, Samuel C. Luckett, Samuel B.T. Caldwell and Joshua Pusey. Nathan Walker was the first president; William Williams was the first Secretary and Treasurer. Williams was also the second president—for *forty* years (1851-1891).

Waterford is famous for its well-preserved state. Less widely appreciated is just how many structures have disappeared over the years.[i] One such casualty is the Laura Page house. The village lost much of its charm when this small two-story stone house was torn down in the 1940s and the stones removed to Leesburg to be used in a house on West Market Street. It was occupied in my childhood by Aunt Laura Page together with her son and grandson, George and Sam. I am glad I can say I knew Aunt Laura, as she was one of only two people I ever knew who had certainly been slaves—the other was Lloyd Curtis. I can remember her as she walked the street, bowed with age and shuffling her feet—it sounded as if she were sifting sand.

During the Civil War, Aunt Laura—then a teenager—had been a slave at the William Cassady farm just east of the village. She later told Cassady descendants how she had hidden in the hay when the Union troops came, fearful of what they would do to her if found. Slave-owners had incentive, of course, to portray Yankee soldiers as marauding barbarians—and there was just enough truth to the charge to keep secessionist whites as well as blacks in a high state of anxiety as the war went against the rebels.

After the war Aunt Laura continued to work for the Cassady family, as well as for the Smith family on the neighboring farm. One of the latter, Eugenia Smith Fred, bequeathed *"one hundred dollars ...to my family servant Laura Page, for her own use, not to be spent by her husband except with her full consent."*[25]

"Ginnie" Smith Fred, by the way, was the third wife of Mr. Frank Fred, who outlived four spouses altogether. More remarkable, three of those wives, including Ginnie, were sisters. The first, Annie, died in childbirth at the Smith farm in 1883 while Frank was off in the Oklahoma Territory running an Indian trading post.[26]

---

[i] Those with long memories can easily count dozens of structures that have disappeared. The actual number is surely much higher when various small outbuildings are included.

The string of houses on Main Street southeast of the Laura Page house has seen some changes over the years. A Dr. E.N. Love came to Waterford shortly after the Civil War and practiced medicine for a time. The story was that he had been a Union surgeon and, in passing through, liked the town and returned shortly after war's end. I believe he lived in the clapboard house next to Aunt Laura's.

A later resident there was Wade Bentley, Waterford's renowned auto mechanic and a real wizard with the old Model T Fords. Most mechanics used tools with insulating wooden or rubber handles when testing the spark plugs and coils. Not Wade. He would touch the hot wire with bare hand, checking the flow of current, seemingly impervious to the charge. Wade also sang bass in an excellent black quartet, together with Clarence Coates from across the street singing tenor and with Hiram Minor from up on the Big Hill and Paul "Scoopum" Mallory accompanying.

The log house that stands next to Wade's old place is a newcomer. It replaces two buildings that burned in the winter of 1965. One had housed the first telephone office in the town. It burned when a resident mistakenly thought he had to keep a hive of bees in his attic from freezing and lit a fire to keep them warm. The other casualty of that blaze was a brick structure built before 1816 by John Williams (1771-1840), one of the town's leading Quaker merchants and father of William Williams. In the 1920s Cressford Divine, son of my Great-Uncle Charlie, had a shoe-repair shop there.

THEODORE MALLORY house, destroyed in 1965 fire.

The present telephone office replaced what had been a small dwelling occupied by Edward (Doc) White,[i] a veteran of the Loudoun Rangers and self-taught horse doctor. Long before, in 1834, William Nettle (1779-1856), a builder from Pennsylvania, had bought the property. The house is known to many as the Sally Nettle house, after William's widow. His executors sold it and an adjoining store in 1880. They were finally demolished or converted in the mid-20th century to make room for the telephone office.

SALLY NETTLE house

The Graham house next door has also seen various uses. It was built about 1810, and in the 1830s Isaac Walker[ii] had a store in the end next to the current post office. This may have been the same store that Isaac was operating with Jacob Mendenhall as early as 1816. A ledger from that period shows that they sold a wide variety of foods and dry goods, from calico to chamber pots.

---

[i] Edward T. White (c.1842-1924). His mother, Sarah Janney White, was a Quaker, and Doc White is buried in Fairfax Cemetery despite his military service.
[ii] Isaac Walker (1781-1851), son of Abel and Mary Branson Walker, married the former Susannah Talbott at Fairfax Meeting in 1812. One of his five children, Mary Elizabeth, became the first wife of William Williams in 1845.

The west end of the building was a dwelling occupied in the 1830s by a John Moore. A later addition to the west end was also used as a store. After the Civil War, Bob Graham, a veteran of Sam Means' Loudoun Rangers, operated from this building as a carriage painter. He did especially fine detail on buggies. Still later, when telephones came to Waterford, the phone company used an annex to the house for storage.

The building on the corner that housed the post office was erected about 1880 on the site of a much earlier structure. Lydia Hollingsworth Hough, daughter-in-law of Old John Hough, apparently built that original building about 1812. Land records refer to it variously as a house or store. John Williams operated a store there in the early 1800s; another Quaker businessman, John B. Dutton, rented the space for his own dry-goods establishment in the 1850s. Dutton's daughter, Mary Frances Dutton Steer, recalled a harrowing episode in three verses of her famous poem *Old Memories*.

> ....*A kindly woman there did live;*
> *We called her "Grandma Reed";*[i]
> *Once when my father's store took fire,*
> *She did a noble deed.*
>
> *She hastened out upon the street,*
> *And hurriedly did call*
> *The powder cans upon the shelf,*
> *Forgotten were by all.*
>
> *The cans so hot were taken down,*
> *And carried from the store,*
> *There was no doubt she saved the town*
> *And no one knows what more....*

As you may have surmised, those cans held gunpowder, not baking powder. The current building has been home to the post office for fully a century now.

---

[i] Amanda Smallwood Reed.

THE OTHER SIDE OF MAIN STREET

Now, if we return to the mill and wend our way again to the center of town, this time on the north or uphill side of Main Street, past the old tanyard, we come first to the brick Richardson-Pierpoint/Ratcliffe house, named for three prominent early owners. Another early resident was Sanford Edmonds, who married Margaret Pierpoint in 1816 after her first husband, Samuel, died. Mr. Edmonds opened a cabinet-making shop in Waterford the following year, but he too met an untimely end about 1825, reportedly from eating too many cherries and swallowing the pits![27]

This building housed Ratcliffe's school in the 1840s. There was also a store building in the side yard, a structure no longer there, though its fireplace remains.

RATCLIFFE HOUSE and store building. The porch, like the store, has been removed.

The large Victorian house encountered next is a relatively recent addition to Main Street—it was built in 1886 by Isaac Steer Hough, Jr., (1840-1915). This house, though, incorporates a much earlier structure, a modest story-and-a-half building that may have been built by one Joseph Pierpoint before he sold the property in 1803.

In this century I remember Isaac Hough's granddaughter, Mary Virginia Hough Davis, and her husband Oscar. He operated a grocery store on the east side of the ground floor. On the west side Mary's cousin Clarice Hough had a millinery shop. At one point, Mary operated the telephone exchange in her home above. That line of work apparently ran in the family. Her sister Lilly Brown was the operator when the exchange was up the street.

The Kitty Leggett house two doors down is one of the older houses on the north side of the street. First mention is made in a deed in a 1791 transfer which mentions "being all of that lot of land situate in Loudoun County in the little town called Waterford whereon Wm Paxson now dwells." This, by the way, is one of the earliest surviving references to the village as Waterford rather than Janney's Mill.

Kitty Leggett must have been interesting; she was twice married, twice widowed, a mother of ten, and illiterate.[i] Like most in the town, she was also a strong Union sympathizer. She organized the young ladies to pass out cookies and greet Union troops as they marched through in 1863 on their way south from Gettysburg. This hospitality from a town in secessionist Virginia obviously made a lasting impression, as the history of the 24th Michigan Infantry makes clear.[28]

> *On July 18th we were back on the sacred soil of Virginia. Near Waterford which to our pleased surprise we found to be a most beautifully embowered and intensely loyal village, a Union oasis in a sea of secession. Rising to the occasion an impromptu dance was held that evening, after the dirt of the day's march was washed off in a clear stream nearby.*

---

[i] Catherine Rinker Wright Liggett (1812-1892). The name was also spelled Leggett as often as not.

According to tradition this dance was held in the street in front of Kitty Leggett's house, where refreshments were handed out. Among the participants was my then 19-year-old grandmother, Sally Roberts.

Some years later, the top floor of this house was damaged by fire, started when a passing steam-powered threshing machine discharged sparks that set the wood shingle roof ablaze.

The fire may also have scorched the Joseph Janney/George Dean house next door. A box of old papers and letters stored against the wall nearest the Leggett house showed burn marks when discovered during a 1980 restoration.

The letters recount how the children of Deacon George Dean had gone to Ohio to work; they were sending back money around 1900 to help pay for their parents' house. In 1992 George's grandson Adolphus Dean returned to the village from Ohio after an absence of some 60 years.

KITTY LEGGETT house and neighbors—before the fire

The house itself goes way back. Joseph Janney, readers may recall, had purchased this lot as part of 12 acres he obtained from Francis Hague's estate in 1781. Since he sold his new house on Bond Street at about the same time, he may have erected this building on Main Street as a replacement. By the time of his death—about 1793—Janney was apparently living on a farm several miles northeast of Waterford.[29]

The stone foundation to the right of Janney's home once supported a small log house that collapsed in the 1970s. For many years in the early part of this century Edward and Marietta Timbers Collins made their home there and raised a family. Numerous descendants still live in the area.[i] Ed and Marietta bought the place in 1909 for $125, and Marietta lived there until shortly before her death in the 1940s. Highly regarded by the whole community, black and white, she had been born to a free black family in Waterford about 1855; she married Mr. Collins around 1870. He had come to the area about 1867, according to information he gave when he registered to vote in 1902.

COLLINS *house*

Ed Collins built the room on the southeast side of the building, as well as the stone retaining wall in front. I remember that he had a good reputation as a "blind ditcher," a builder of stone culverts and underground drainage in those days before plastic pipe. His co-worker and close friend was Charlie Virts,[ii] a veteran of the Loudoun Rangers.

There is good evidence that Ed himself was a veteran of the war, although in his later years the family was unable to convince government

---

[i] Some of the cottage's history was brought to light in 1993 by Dan Kent of Loudoun County High School and his team of student archeologists.
[ii] Charles W. Virts (1845-1940).

pension officials.[i] According to the family, he was a survivor of the massacre by Confederates at Fort Pillow, Tennessee, in April 1864. Later, in the early 1900s, as a drummer with other Waterford musicians, he enjoyed traveling to Washington to hear John Philip Sousa concerts.

A story was told that Ed worked for William Paxson on a nearby farm, and that one day he did not feel up to going to work. Paxson came looking for him. Ed's son Leeford answered the door, and Paxson inquired about his father and was he home? Leeford said he was. To which the usually hard-working Ed responded, *"Leeford, 'name of God, why didn't you think your thoughts and tell the man I wasn't home?"*

MARIETTA COLLINS,
on her birthday, circa 1940

---

[i] Descendants remember "Grandfather's uniform and gun behind the door." The archeological dig at the site in 1993 turned up a Civil War uniform button and buckle.

My Great-Uncle Charlie had a shoe shop just to the right of the Collins house. Even less remains of this building, once the center of much activity during the Civil War. Charles Divine[i] was one of the few who subscribed to a newspaper (the *Baltimore American*), which drew villagers to read the paper, loaf, and exchange the news of the day. On April 10, 1865, the big news was of General Lee's surrender the day before. My family always told that several Quakers were in the shop when the paper with the joyful news arrived, and they, forgetting the tenets of their Meeting, grabbed each other and danced all over the shop.

This account is not far-fetched; Quakers in neighboring Goose Creek (now Lincoln) showed similar exuberance. Moses Pascal Watson ran a mill at Guinea Bridge that was burned by General Sheridan's men in 1864. But his wife hid the mill ledger in the dog house and thus saved it. Here is the entry for Thursday, April 13, 1865:

> *There is great rejoicing with the Union people in regards to the fall of Richmond [and] the surrender of Gen. Lee. It is said Samuel M. Janney had the old Gobbler killed and invited many of his Union friends to eat and be merry. William Tate shut himself up in a room and laughed his fill. Joseph Nichols has been riding hunting [up] hands to go to his house and drink cider. Bill Lemon and Lot Tavenner is gone fishing today, they say the work is done....*

Uncle Charlie made shoes for many customers. One man, a slave owner nearby,[ii] was said to march his slaves in from the farm and have them measured for summer shoes and then, in the fall, he would repeat the operation for winter boots.

Just up from Uncle Charlie's shop then and now is a row of attached buildings near the center of town that served, at various times, both residential and commercial purposes.

---

[i] Charles William Divine (1823-1906).
[ii] William Cassady (also spelled Cassaday), owner of *Oakland* farm east of town.

The three-story brick building anchoring the northwest end of the joined structures was used first as a dwelling. Then in 1850 it became a hall for the Odd Fellows of Evergreen Lodge 51, then again a dwelling. Next door there was and is a second residence, and adjoining that is a building long used as a tavern. I never heard an accurate account of how the floor plan of this public place was arranged, but I believe that the street level was used for the bar and meeting rooms. In another verse from *Old Memories*, Molly Steer expressed some thoughts about this building:

> *A Tavern stood upon the street*
> *That some did much deplore*
> *For many a noble-minded man*
> *Went down to rise no more.*

She was probably not exaggerating. Waterford's historical record is full of allusions to what we would call alcoholism. Even Ms. Steer's Quakers were known to overimbibe, though they did so at peril to their standing with the meeting. The minutes of Fairfax Meeting all too commonly chronicle "excessive drinking of spiritous liquors" and complain of members "being disguised with strong drink."[30] Still, the Quakers did not officially back abstinence until the formation of the Friends Temperance Union in 1852. So we should not be too surprised that an inventory of the estate of the cultivated Asa Moore in 1823 included some 72 beer bottles, four decanters and 15 wine glasses.[31]

By 1852, by the way, Waterford had already had for some years its own branch of the Sons of Temperance.[32] And at the end of that century the Anti-Saloon League would gather liquor, pray over it at a meeting hall on Second Street, and with great ceremony pour it into the creek. They sang hymns as it flowed away. For all their efforts none of these organizations won the battle with the bottle.

ROW HOUSES. Arch House on right.

The tavern had ceased operation before my time, but I remember playing in the basement or street level of the building, and there were meat hooks attached to the walls, indicating that it had been a store or meat market at some time.

Local businessmen met in the tavern in early 1815 to organize the Loudoun Company and elect officers. Once this bank was up and running, as I have mentioned, the directors moved their meetings across the street to more sober quarters befitting a financial institution.

Later in the 1920s the telephone office, or switchboard, was located in the room next to the *Arch House*. I remember that if you were going to be away for a few hours, you called the operator to tell her, and she would know not to ring your house when a call came for you.

The adjoining *Arch House* was built as part of the same tavern building in 1809/10. It provided living quarters overhead and a street-level store. The arched passage off the street gave access to a well in the rear. Fire ladders and buckets for town use were stored in the arch as a protection against the weather. This use of the archway exempted the owner from town taxes.

I mention the next house, toward the center of town from the *Arch House*, because of its interesting early use—originally as one story—as John Williams' iron storage house. Mr. Williams stored his inventory of bar iron here as an annex to his general merchandise store across the street on the site of the post office. A recent occupant of the *Arch House* once told me that, in making repairs to his east side, which abutted the store house, he found weatherboarding next to the *Arch House*, indicating that the store house had been built before its neighbor. Surprising.

The Town Council

Well before Main Street was fully developed, the citizens of the growing town saw a need for a bit of self-regulation. They wanted to improve the health and safety of residents and provide other amenities for the common good. To meet that need the Commonwealth of Virginia in 1801 established a board of trustees to see to Waterford's public business.

We have only indirect knowledge of the ordinances and other measures the board put in place, but we know something about the four trustees themselves: The Williams brothers, John and Abner, were Quakers who had long been in the area,[i] as was James Moore, who had come with his parents from Pennsylvania in 1780. The fourth, James Griffith, also appears to have had family links to Fairfax Meeting.

Waterford continued to expand in the decades that followed, drawing its prosperity from the fertile, well-managed farms in the vicinity. In 1818, an act of the Commonwealth General Assembly enlarged the town to its present outlines,[33] and by the mid-1830s a newly published Virginia gazetteer described it as a "fine flourishing little village," surrounded by wheat and corn land "equal to any in the state."[34] The author offered statistics to support his glowing assessment.

> *Waterford contains 70 dwelling houses, 2 houses of public worship, 1 free for all denominations, the other a Friends' meeting house, 6 mercantile stores, 2 free schools, 4 taverns, 1 manufacturing flour mill, and 1 saw, grist and plaister mill, and (in the vicinity) 2 small cotton manufactories. The mechanics are 1 tanner, 2 house joiners, 2 cabinet makers, 1 chair maker and painter, 1 boot and shoe manufacturer, 2 hatters, 1 tailor, &c. Population about 400 persons; of whom 3 are regular physicians.*

Clearly, this little village had become a place of some significance—it was the second largest town in Loudoun County, a distinction it held for the rest of the century. And just as clearly it was time for more substantial governing arrangements. Accordingly, on March 22, 1836, the

---

[i] John Williams (1771-1840) and his brother Abner (1773-1851) were sons of William Williams, the elder, who had married Elizabeth Everett at Fairfax Meeting in 1769.

town was incorporated. Three commissioners duly elected nine councilmen and on May 18, William Nettle, the builder, became the first mayor. Israel Griffith was appointed recorder and Oscar Reed the first town sergeant.[i]

The councilmen rolled up their sleeves and went to work. The first order of business was to redraft the ordinances of the 1801 commissioners and make a few changes. "Immorality and other irregularities" were again discouraged, residents were granted a more leisurely 48 hours (instead of 24) to remove obstructions and nuisances from the streets and alleys, and the fine for removing fire hooks, ladders and other implements was reduced from $20 to $5. The men also altered regulations regarding "shews, exhibitions...and cock fights," though we do not know the particulars.

The following month the council established a board of health and set up taxes to pay for lime to be distributed among the citizens for "the purpose of whitewashing and liming cellars and other places which may require purification." Evidently the townspeople did not always avail themselves of this free disinfectant, so a few years later the council formed a committee to go around in the first week of July, August, and September to examine cellars for "any nuisance that might be detrimental to the health of the community." In September 1836 they also ordered that "no body be interred in the town limits." There were already two cemeteries for that purpose, that of the Quakers and another for everyone else—the Union of Churches Cemetery.

By November of that year, the councilmen had a more prosaic concern—comfortable chairs for their meetings. They bought nine (for a total of $5.18), perhaps from John Mount, who had set up shop in the village in 1827. Mount made a stylish and serviceable ladder-back, splint-seated model that we know today as a "Waterford chair."

The minutes of the council's meetings show that bureaucracy in Loudoun County is not new. Then as now the all-purpose solution to every issue was a fresh committee, whether to procure chairs or to "examine the situation of Market [Main] Street near the Market House

---

[i] The commissioners were John Braden, Joshua Pusey and Samuel Harris; the councilmen were William Nettle, Israel T. Griffith, Jonathan Cost, Edward Coghlin, Asa and Edward Bond, Ephraim Schooley, Lewis Coale, and Moses Janney.

and superintend the necessary repairs thereof" or "to examine the foot pavements on Market Street and report such repairs as may be necessary."

Bridging Catoctin Creek

The council appears not to have concerned itself with an appeal in May 1838 for a bridge over Catoctin Creek at the north end of town—this was a matter for the county. Thomas Phillips, the miller, and 127 other heads of household in the village and northward petitioned the county for a crossing that would be safe for travelers and their wagons and possessions at times of high water. This petition, the third on that issue, was finally successful.

In June 1838, the county appropriated $2,000 to bridge the creek. The new crossing was 65 feet long, framed with massive 12 by 14-inch white pine runners and girders. To preserve the structure from the elements the builders roofed it with wood shingles and sheathed the sides with oak weatherboard.

The bridge was built well and it served the community for 50 years. Its eventual undoing was the torrential rain that caused the disastrous Johnstown Flood in Pennsylvania. During the night of May 30, 1889, the bridge went down in roiling waters. According to my father, who was 16 at the time, there were no eyewitnesses, "*but the Brown brothers near the mill heard it go over. Debris was scattered over the meadows below but most of it went not over a mile.*"

Over the years the council met in a number of buildings. Their founding minutes described the corporation "in Common Hall assembled." The first year they were meeting in the room over the shop of Moses Janney; in 1837 and 1838 elections for a new mayor and council were held at the home of Ann Paxson, a widow who lived on Main Street.[i] Later, once the Market House was repaired, meetings could be held there. In its final years the council convened above L.P. Smith's mortuary on Second Street, formerly the chair manufactory of his father-in-law Lewis N. Hough.

The town record falls silent after May 1839. In fact, according to leading citizen and keen observer William Williams, the village had begun to lose some of its earlier momentum. Until *"the year 1820 Waterford increased rapidly and promised fair to become a place of some note...But as every unnatural stimulus is followed by great prostration, it suddenly ceased to improve about that time and has ever since* [Williams was writing about 1860] *presented the appearance of a finished city."*[ii]

While "great prostration" might have been overstating the facts, growth had indeed leveled off. In a court deposition in 1836 involving William Nettle and Noble S. Braden, executor of his father Robert's considerable estate, the younger Braden argued that property prices in the town had been severely depressed since his father's death nine years earlier and that Waterford was *"a declining village."*[35]

One index of the reduced pace of development can be found in a survey of the town by James Oden commissioned in 1875. (Several of the maps in this book are drawn from that source.) So little has changed from that day to this that property lines shown on Oden's map are easily matched to the aerial photograph of the village made in 1996.

The town's incorporation lasted a full 100 years, but it could not survive the Great Depression. In 1936, faced with the county's insistence that the village pave its own streets with monies not available, the council unincorporated. A member[iii] of the last town council recalled that the council did borrow $2,800 to pave the rough and dusty main streets. But

---

[i] Ann Shawen Paxson (c.1799-c.1850). Her husband John Paxson had died in 1835.
[ii] From an essay on the *History of Waterford, Virginia*, published by the Friends Literary Society of Waterford 1857-1860. It is initialed "WW" and is generally attributed to Williams.
[iii] Douglas N. Myers (1896-1982).

that money was eventually repaid out of a fund appropriated by Loudoun's Board of Supervisors, part of the profits from liquor sold in the county.

VIEW OF TOWN CENTER, c.1915. Visible from left on far (north) side of Main Street are the Pink House, Paxson's Store, Johnson's Corner, the ticket office, and the Town Hall.

Town Center

Once again I have got ahead of myself—the development of much of the center of town comes first. The most prominent building in that part of the village today is the *Pink House*. In my time it was Mr. Burr Paxson's[i] dwelling over a store and Heber Schooley's barber shop.

I had a never-to-be-forgotten experience in that shop. I was very small, waiting my turn in the chair. The occupant of the chair was a man, Billy Steer,[iii] who was terribly retarded. While harmless, he frightened every boy in town with the guttural sounds he made trying to talk. This day, as he attempted to get out of the chair, he fell forward and his head went through the window, shattering glass everywhere. Blood flowed freely, and out the door I went in a hurry. I was so panic-stricken that when I reached home, I had trouble telling my mother why I came home without a haircut.

> During the Civil War, incidentally, Billy Steer unwittingly helped save his brother Frank from Confederate conscription. The Steers were Quakers and—in accordance with their faith—nonbelligerents, although their sympathies lay strongly with the Union. Since 1861 Frank had managed to dodge rebel conscriptors, but on March 7, 1865, three Confederates appeared unexpectedly at the house on Second Street and demanded the "young man that was in there." While Frank fled up the kitchen stair, his sister-in-law managed to persuade the rebels that the man they had spotted in the house was just Billy, who was clearly unfit for service.[36]
>
> Shortly after the war, young diarist Marie Matthews recorded how Billy had ridden up one day to deliver the mail. He was pretending to be Confederate cavalry officer E.V. "Lige" White[ii]—long a scourge of Waterford Quakers. Clearly the war had made a lasting, if confused, impression on him.

---

[i] Burr W. Paxson (1846-1925) was a great-grandson of William Paxson (1764-1846), who lived in the Kitty Leggett house in 1791.
[ii] Lt. Col. Elijah Viers White (1832-1907), commander of the 35th Battalion Virginia Cavalry.
[iii] William E. Steer (1833-1919), son of James M. and Elizabeth Pancoast Steer.

These days it would be hard to imagine Waterford without the Pink House but the old building has had at least one close call. Terry Hirst, a leading Loudoun businessman and county official for much of this century, once told me that he had wanted to buy the house for its bricks, which the county would use to build a new structure in Leesburg. But the bricks were too soft so the sale fell through.

From Dust to Dust: Waterford's Brick

Much of Waterford's old brick is just as soft as that in the Pink House. It was made of clay dug from along Catoctin Creek and fired nearby. Many buildings, like the old mill, have had to have deteriorating walls and chimneys restored; others are still in need of repair. One clever preservation technique involves carefully removing eroded bricks and re-laying them with their damaged faces turned inward, away from the elements.

Of course there is not always enough left to make that possible. One contemporary of mine remembered making mud pies at one house and scooping red dust from the soft brick to make icing for her cakes.

I believe bricks were used first in Waterford for chimneys. The early settlers built chiefly of log and stone, materials more readily at hand. Brick apparently did not come into common use for entire houses in the village until shortly before 1800. Of course it was out of the question to haul large loads of brick over the rough roads of the day, so the villagers had to make their own.

The clay for the first small batches was probably dug from pits along the creek at the north end of town, a couple of hundred yards downstream from the mill—shallow depressions were still visible in the ground there when I was a child. After 1812, though, when brick houses began going up along Second Street, brickyards were opened closer to the building sites. There was one behind the Isaac Walker house (near Church Street extended to the millrace) and a larger one behind the Mahlon Schooley house—just north of Mahlon Street if it were extended to the race.

These yards opened a new era in Waterford and gave it a construction impetus that caused many to think the village would become a large town. The old brick houses along Second Street that survive today date from the "building boom" of about 1810-1825.

Mr. Paxson's property included the *Pink House*, a store, and a two-story frame building with a meeting hall on the second floor. This building, now gone, was known as the Town Hall, or Paxson's Hall. It was attached to the store at a right angle. The space in front of the intersection had a southeastern exposure, making an excellent loafing place in all kinds of weather. Between the hall and the store was a small 8 by 10 room intended to be a ticket office for community events. Mr. Fenton Paxson rented this room as his private loafing place—he had a kerosene stove there for cold days. Fent was Burr Paxson's cousin and yet another veteran of the Loudoun Rangers.

"LOITERING PERMITTED"—Johnson's Corner

The Hall was the center of activity over the years. It would hold about 100—when people stood at the rear. Today's fire marshals would have had cardiac arrest at the people crowded into that tinderbox.

Oh! what memories that old hall brings to mind. Plays and minstrel shows graced its stage, War Bond rallies were held there during World War I, and of course the medicine shows. All the town "plays" were held there. The dressing rooms were tiny, and any time there was a large cast, everyone had to breathe in unison. On one occasion, the hero made a grand entrance by stumbling over a suitcase and landing head first, prone, on stage. The seats were wooden chairs with "Piedmont Cigarettes" in large letters on the backs. Most performances were punctuated by the collapse of at least one of those chairs.

But the greater excitement was when a Medicine Show came to town. To those uninitiated, the medicine shows entertained with stage acts, then sold patent medicine. As I look back, it was pretty "sick" comedy, but when I compare the shows with some of the current television presentations, they fare tolerably well.

The interesting parts were the two intermissions when they peddled their drugs. **DR. WELLS' WONDER HERB CURE** was one of these. To hear the sales pitch, you'd believe this elixir would cure everything from dandruff to flat feet. It contained about 75 percent alcohol, and a couple of slugs would deaden any pain. Many people swore by it until the effects of two bottles wore off, and by that time the show had left town.

MEDICINE SHOW *entertainers*

While talking about entertainment, I most remember the tent shows that came to the schoolhouse field and stayed five days. Some had a couple of animals, usually a toothless lion or tiger, and always a monkey or two. One time a monkey got loose and was caught and returned by a local man who cornered it in a barn. I was too young to go on the monkey detail, but the idea thrilled me. The most popular tent show, and one that came for several years, was RIPPLE BROS. They had a catchy slogan: **Not a Ripple but a Splash in an Ocean of Mirth**. Those who missed those days missed a lot of life as Waterford knew it.

All school activities, plays, graduations and the like, were held in Paxson's hall until the school auditorium was built in 1928 by my father, J. Elbert Divine, and a Mr. Kelly, a contractor for the school board. Paxson's Hall was torn down in the early 1930s; the materials were "recycled" as a farm building a few miles west of Waterford.[i] This is a new term for an old practice once common in a poorer, more frugal America.

The former store building was converted into a dwelling. During a hard thunderstorm in the 1930s, a flood of water came down the bank, inundating the living space. The occupants escaped, and the husband, maintaining his sense of humor, commented that, *"I have the most modern house in Waterford—running water in every room."*

At the east end of the hall, while it stood, was "Doc" White's horse hospital. Mr. Ed White, as mentioned earlier, lived across the street. He was a self-taught veterinarian who probably learned his trade while a member of Sam Means' cavalry. The two-stall building was used when he needed to keep a horse for observation, otherwise he had "office hours": that is when the farmer brought his animal for immediate treatment. I believe this small barn had originally been part of a stable the tavern used for the convenience of overnight guests.

---

[i] Will Peacock owned the farm, later part of the Legard estate.

DOC WHITE & ROBERT B. HOUGH, brothers-in-law

Adjoining the barn was Mr. Noble Robinson's[i] Ice Cream Parlor. "Uncle Nobe" was open for business on weekends, selling oysters in the winter and ice cream in the warmer months. He served delicious ice cream in generous portions; for a nickel, a little boy could almost get filled up.

Uncle Nobe's log house, at the foot of Water Street, has come to be called the *Weavers Cottage*. I never heard that name until recent times. He was not a weaver and I do not believe the name was in use in his time. But a relative, William Robinson, purchased the house in 1854 from a weaver named Charles Hammer, who lived there with his wife Mary, so maybe the term dates from that period. The Hammers, by the way, were immigrants from Germany.[37]

---

[i] African-American Noble Robinson (c.1846-c.1928) was the son of Nancy Robinson who was born about 1814. Family documents link her to William Lane, born free about 1785.

Two more houses completed the development along Water Street of six lots sold by William Hough's heirs after 1815.[i] Neither was livable in my memory. One belonged to Nathan Minor's heirs. The other, I had heard, had been owned by Alfred Craven (b. 1830), teamster for William Williams' fine team of horses. Now reduced to a pile of rubble just east of the *Weavers Cottage*, it was later occupied by Malinda Rucker, a lady who loved roses to the extent they filled her back yard.

Malinda Curtis had married Clifton Rucker about 1884 and raised a large family. Most of her nine children went to New York to work, but son Jim stayed on and worked for years in the Waterford area. Daughter Nora's own daughter, Sarah Rucker Gordon, shared much about early 20th-century life in the black community. Malinda was a midwife in Waterford; she also took in summer boarders.

WATER STREET, THE TOWN TRIANGLE & MAIN STREET HILL, c. 1910.
Visible at left are the Weavers Cottage and the Craven/Rucker & Minor houses.

---

[i] See, for example, Loudoun County Deed Book 3S, pp. 306-307 for a description of the sale of Lot Number 4, sold to Nathan Minor.

The Corner Store at the intersection of Second and Main Streets held center stage in Waterford's commercial life for more than half a century. I will speak only of the period from about 1900 to World War II, although there had been a store there years before.

OLD CORNER STORE. *The frail figure at right is said to be Lewis N. Hough (1829-1900).*

About 1878, owner Lemuel P. Smith came to Waterford from Dranesville to marry Ella Hough, daughter of Lewis N. Hough, a successful chair and coffin manufacturer in the village. Lem Smith stayed in the town and for four decades did much for it as a merchant, mortician, churchman, town councilman, and participant in any activity that benefited the area.

Long before the advent of malls, these small town stores carried nearly every necessity for daily living. From clothing to canned goods, from candles to kerosene, Mr. Smith had it all. He also took in country butter and eggs for credit. In lieu of a few pennies, school kids could exchange a couple of eggs for candy at the noon break.

Visitors to Waterford no doubt find it strange that this—or any—building should be standing over a small creek, but the store was at the junction of four important streets, and this particular creek—the Town Branch—doesn't flood all that often. The store's elevation had another disadvantage for Mr. Smith, however, for one night a barrel of sugar was stolen. This feat was accomplished by the thief's standing in the stream beneath where a recently arrived barrel of sugar stood. With a drill, he bored through the store floor and then through the barrel. It was then a simple matter for him to catch the sugar as it poured down through the hole.

For several years, Mr. Smith rented the closed Paxson's store during the holiday season and used it as a Christmas store. Oh! What a thrill it was to see so many things near and dear to a little boy's heart. There were little red wagons, sleighs and tricycles, then, for the girls, dolls and games. No mall today can give the pleasure of that little Christmas store. When the holiday was over, there were no after-season sales. Mr. Smith simply packed everything away and set it out again the next year to thrill us all over again.

L. P. Smith

Dealer in

Dry Goods, Notions, Hardware, Boots, Shoes
Rubber Goods, Cigars and Tobacco

Glass, Queensware, &c.

WAR STORIES

I drove Mr. Smith to Point of Rocks several times to meet his daughter who visited from her home in Pittsburgh. This was a pleasure, as he talked of the Civil War. He had been nine years old at the outbreak and had an excellent memory of events. He told me of his youth at Dranesville and of seeing marching troops. One summer night in 1863 he heard J.E.B. Stuart's cavalry pass on their way to Gettysburg.

Through the 1920s and into the early 1930s Mr. Smith's Corner Store porch was a gathering place at mail time for several old Civil War veterans of the Union army. These "Yankees" were no longer fighting "Rebels," but disagreement among themselves often broke out, with resultant shouting and cane-thumping.

Mr. Robert W. "Cripple Bob" Hough would go home, and fume (as we would hear from my Aunt Dolly, at whose home he boarded), "*I don't know what's wrong with Joe [my grandfather, Joseph T. Divine]. He is all wrong about the war.*" Meanwhile, Grandfather Divine would go home and complain to my Aunt Clara, "*I don't know what's wrong with Bob. You can't tell him anything.*" Despite their disagreements, they were right back the next day, ready to resume their private war. There were a couple of Confederate veterans around, but they stayed out of these bouts.

Joseph T. Divine

The war affected later generations as well, including Aunt Dolly and Aunt Clara. Aunt Dolly, born Florence Virginia Mullen, was my mother's older sister. Unmarried, she dedicated most of her 84 years (1863-1947) to helping others. Many Waterford households could bear testimony to her kindness in times of trouble, illness, or death. She was always there, helping the needy.

The war was over before she was old enough to remember, but those who kept reliving it left a strong impression: Aunt Dolly loved everybody except Abraham Lincoln and Yankees. Even as an old lady, her dislike for Lincoln never abated. In passing the Lincoln Memorial in Washington, she would turn her head. And she would say she would not take a five dollar bill unless forced to.

While she never voted, she was an ardent Democrat; I think she was more anti-Lincoln. She ran a boarding house on the Big Hill diagonally across the street from the Methodist Church.[i] Life is full of ironies and it didn't spare Aunt Dolly, for her boarder with the longest tenure, as I have mentioned, was "Cripple Bob" Hough, the thrice-wounded veteran of the Union army.

When she was 80, we took her to the Gettysburg battlefield. Unable to get out of the car, she sat looking at the equestran statue of General Lee, and, with tears running down her cheeks, she said, *"Poor old Robert, he did all he could."*

Unreconstructed to the end.

Aunt Clara Divine (1872-1936) was my father's older sister. She, like Aunt Dolly, was ever willing to help others in times of trouble, sickness and death. Aunt Clara found many ways to contribute to small-town life. She and Aunt Dolly got along fine if the war was not mentioned. But her dislike for Southern soldiers and Democrats equaled Aunt Dolly's hatred of the Republicans.

One time Aunt Clara went to the local precinct to vote. The policy was for the judge —or election official—to hand the voter a ballot to be marked. When the ballot was completed, it was returned to the judge, who deposited it in the box. But on this occasion, when Aunt Clara marked her ballot and the Democratic judge reached for it, she snapped, *"Oh no you don't! I don't trust any Democrat."*

The judge went home and told his wife of Aunt Clara's insult. The lady wrote her a letter saying, *"I resent what you said to my husband as I am a Southern-bread [sic] woman."* Aunt Clara snorted, *"She spells just like an ignorant Democrat!"*

Two gallant ladies who never forgot.

---

[i] Aunt Dolly lived in the George Schooley house on the north side of the Hill, next to Lloyd Curtis's house.

A Few More War Stories

Many others in Waterford found it hard to forget. The physical and social wounds inflicted during four hard years of war left deep scars on the village and its residents. Some never healed.

I have written elsewhere of the wider war and its effect on this small town in the border area between north and south—particularly its impact on the anti-secessionist Quakers.[i] I do not propose to refight the same battles here. But a few accounts and stories from other perspectives may give the reader some flavor of the times and help explain why it was so hard for the survivors of those days—and even their children—to let the past lie.

The war was terrible enough by any standard. It was doubly so for Waterford for two reasons: First, the area was deeply divided on the issues of slavery and secession. While most of the villagers were overwhelmingly pro-Union, many of their neighbors and most of the county as a whole were just as fervently secessionist.

Second, the war would not go away. The town changed hands repeatedly between 1861 and 1865, and though the local clashes were relatively small, they were nonetheless deadly. Often it was neighbor against neighbor.

In at least one celebrated case it was literally brother against brother—William and Charles Snoots, to be precise. William was a sergeant in Maj. Elijah V. White's 35th Battalion Virginia Cavalry; Charles had joined the pro-Union Loudoun Rangers led by Capt. Sam Means, Waterford's former miller.

At dawn on August 27, 1862, White's men launched a surprise attack on the Rangers, who were bivouacked at the Baptist Church. In a bloody three-hour fire-fight the rebels forced the trapped and outgunned Rangers to accept a conditional surrender. William Snoots, his blood still up, tried to shoot his captured brother Charles but was "rebuked by his officers for such an unsoldierly and unbrotherly desire."[38] It is a wonder both boys survived the war.

---

[i] See Divine, Souders & Souders, *"To Talk Is Treason,"* Waterford Foundation, 1996.

In the same clash, incidentally, the senior Union officer on the scene, Lt. Luther Slater, was wounded in the temple, shoulder, arm, chest, and hand—not to mention a carbine ball that passed through his hat. Remarkably, he eventually recovered, thanks in no small part to concerned neighbors. A month after the battle, when Slater was still too ill to travel by horse or carriage, some ten of them "came and fastened a pole to each side of his rocking chair, in which position they carried him [5 miles!] to his father's residence near Taylorstown."[39]

Because churches typically were large, sturdy buildings that happened to be suitable for quartering troops, they were often commandeered for that purpose. Waterford's Quaker Meeting House had been put to that use by Confederate cavalry the previous winter, much to the consternation of the strictly pacifist congregation.

FAIRFAX MEETING HOUSE

A vivid first-hand account of that episode survives. Susan Walker, daughter of James and Eliza Hunt Walker of Talbott Farm on the southern edge of the village, presented the following essay to a literary society at Earlham College in Indiana during the 1862-63 term. She was 17 years old at the time and a student at the college.

A Quaker Meeting in Dixie[40]

It was a beautiful morning in the winter of 1861, when the Friends of Fairfax Meeting began to assemble at the usual hour around the old stone meeting house.

Great was their surprise upon arriving there, to find that it was occupied by two companies of Confederate Cavalry, that had encamped during the previous night. Some of the oldest and most influential Friends immediately sought out the Captains and told them of their situation, that the house was their place of worship, and that there had not been a meeting missed for over one hundred years and if the arrangement could possibly be made, they would be obliged for the use of the house for at least two hours.

At first the officers thought it would be impossible, but after some consultation concluded the building was large enough for them all, and said if the Friends would wait awhile they could make some room for them. So the women sat in the carriages while the men entered the house and assisted the soldiers to pack their bedding and baggage to one side. The partition[i] *was soon closed and those of the soldiers who did not wish to attend the meeting were sent into the other side of the house.*

However, almost all had curiosity to be present, having heard of Quaker Meetings. When the members entered, the scenes presented there were strange ones for the interior of a Friends Meeting House, and had it not been for the solemnity of the occasion would have been truly amusing. The old ladies ascended the steps into the gallery and took their seats, though rather daintily,

---

[i] Fairfax Meeting House had a partition that would be rolled down from wooden drums in the ceiling to divide the open room for men's and women's business meetings. Two of these reels survive.

as arms were stacked behind them, muskets and swords stored away beneath the benches.

In one corner of the room the "Stars and Bars" were unfurled. In an opposite one was a large fireplace with a blazing fire, over which was roasting a large turkey, also some hominy cooking. Overcoats were hanging all about, knapsacks and saddles were strewn around, while a suppressed titter or an amused whisper of some of the more mischievous soldiers regarding the peculiar shape of the plain bonnets could be distinctly heard.

But when all were seated it was perfectly quiet, and when an aged and feeble lady[i] rose every countenance wore a thoughtful aspect and each attentively listened to her words of truth and love. When she invoked a blessing on the little band there assembled, she also prayed that the wings of peace might be spread over our once prosperous and happy land, also for the strangers that were that day gathered in their midst, until loud sobs broke from strong men and great tears forced themselves down their sunburnt cheeks.

After meeting many of them expressed their gratification of having been allowed to assemble with the members, and said they hoped to have another opportunity. Of course, the Friends were not desirous that they should remain in the house but invited them to attend their meetings whenever they felt inclined.

Since that day there have been many assemblings for worship in the same room and amid the same military surroundings. They have been mostly solemn and impressive, but different from our nice, quiet little ones at Earlham.

Those who have not been surrounded by war and its attendant horrors, know but poorly how to appreciate the almost perfect peace and tranquillity that reigns here. I hope never again to hear the familiar sound of booming cannons or noise of musketry, and that ere I return to the Blue Ridge Hills of my native state they will have passed forever from our land.

---

[i] This was probably Miriam Taylor Gover (1791-1863), a respected meeting elder for many years.

Another vexing consequence of the war for young women like Susan Walker was the absence of virtually all the eligible men of their generation. When a soldier of the right stripe *did* happen by, it was an opportunity not to be missed, even in less than ideal circumstances. Briscoe Goodhart, veteran and chronicler of the Loudoun Rangers, recounted one such episode.[41]

On Monday, May 17, 1863, the Rangers fell into a trap set by John S. Mosby's rebel partisans just south of town. Several were killed and wounded. *Those of our boys that were made prisoners were marched back through Waterford. Miss ———, one of the many loyal ladies of that burg, and perhaps the most demonstrative, kissed Sergt. James H. Beatty, which made the mouths of Mosby's men water, but it was to no avail, as Miss ——— was a little particular who she kissed.*

The prisoners were marched on through Hamilton and Upperville. That night, near Piedmont Station, Sergt. James H. Beatty made a break for liberty. He darted through the woods in the darkness like a greyhound. About a hundred shots were fired after him, but he went faster than the bullets. It was less than two months since he returned from Belle Isle Prison [Richmond], that "hell on earth." The thoughts of so soon returning nerved him to outrun greased lightning. He traveled all night and part of the next day, and the next night arrived at Waterford, greatly to the delight of his friends. He repaid Miss ____ with double compound interest, the kiss she so ungrudgingly bestowed thirty-six hours before. It was a clear case on Miss ____'s part of casting "bread upon the waters."

Loudoun Rangers reunion

Unfortunately, few stories of that war took such a happy turn. Take the case of Capt. Charles F. Anderson, whose family lived a couple of miles north of Waterford on the road to Taylorstown. He and his son Fleming had both joined the Loudoun Rangers in June 1862. Capt. Anderson met an inglorious end on November 1, 1863, when he slipped and fell some 200 feet to his death from his unit's camp on Magazine Heights near Harpers Ferry.[42] My grandfather who was with him in camp wrote home that Anderson had been *"a little tight...but there is a great many of the boys that think he was pushed over there by some one."*[43]

The following year, Sgt. Fleming Anderson was celebrating Christmas eve at his widowed mother's when the house was surrounded by 16 of White's and Mosby's rebels. The young soldier made a break for the back door but caught his saber on the back of his chair and was shot trying to free it. "In falling, his mother caught him in her arms, and he died in a few minutes."[44]

On the other side, the pain experienced by families of the Confederate dead and maimed was at least as great. Not only were their husbands, fathers, and sons lost, but *The Cause* as well.

Everyone suffered the scarcities and disruptions of four years of war. Waterford itself had narrowly escaped being torched by the rebels in 1862. The Baptist Church was so badly damaged in White's raid that same year that two years after Lee's surrender its members were still debating its fate. *"Some of the members are in favor of selling it. Some want to repair [it]."*[45] It did not reopen until 1876.

The greatest blow to the local economy, though, was Gen. Phil Sheridan's methodically executed "burning order" of November 1864. In an effort to starve the rebel partisans out of Loudoun County, Union troops seized or burned virtually everything—other than houses—of potential value to the enemy.

Sgt. Joseph T. Divine

Ghosts

Aunt Dolly devoted much of her later life to taking care of her mother after the death of Grandfather in 1903. She never lost her love for her Baptist Church nor her belief in ghosts. Woe be unto anyone who did not share her belief in the supernatural.

I enjoyed hearing Aunt Dolly's stories but, never having seen a ghost, remained privately skeptical. Several years after her death, though, I had an experience that is still as fresh in my mind as the day it shook me.

On January 24, 1885, Landon Merchant, a man who lived north of Waterford, was found dead on the road that leads to Clark's Gap; his white horse was standing near the body. Mr. Merchant's head had suffered a severe blow, whether from a fall from his horse or foul play was not known, but a legend was born of the "Man on the White Horse."

Aunt Dolly, herself, had seen the white horse, and in an unpleasant way, resulting in skinned shins. She and several others of the younger set were going to a party in a light wagon with boards across the wagon bed for additional seats. As they passed the site of Merchant's death, their horses shied to the side, and a white horse reared up, striking the board in front of Aunt Dolly and driving it back into her shins. I recall that she *did* have a badly scarred leg.

There is a sequel. In 1964, while doing an article for the Waterford Foundation, I interviewed Miss Eleanor "Bide" Chamberlin.[i] This was a great experience as Miss Eleanor, then 90 years old, was a charming lady with an excellent memory of her life at *Clifton* on Clark's Gap Road and the stories her mother had related of Civil War times there. Each trip to visit her was such a pleasure that I'll admit that I made more than were necessary for the article. Talking to her and her niece, Mrs. Edith Stahl, was unforgettable.

One day, when I was leaving, Miss Bide said, *"John, why don't you write about the Man on the White Horse?"*

---

[i] Eleanor Chamberlin, "Bide"—pronounced "BYdee," was one of two sisters of Edward, Paul, Justin and Leroy Chamberlin, all children of Edith Matthews and Col. Simon Elliott Chamberlin.

I was bug-eyed. Shades of Aunt Dolly! Seventeen years after her death I hear of the Man on the White Horse from another source. My question to Miss Bide: *"Did you ever see it?"*

"No, but my brother and others saw it many years ago."

With testimonials from persons of the character of these two ladies, maybe we should take a second look at ghosts.

Of course every churchyard has its stories, and one of these involves Fairfax Meeting. During World War I, people reported seeing a spectral "woman in black," wandering around the grounds, always in or near the shed used to shelter horses during services. Neighbors finally decided that the woman, whom they recognized as one living just beyond the village, was extremely anxious about the absence of her husband in the army and somehow felt reassured being in that place. But forever etched on my mind was the morning that I heard an old Civil War veteran say, *"The woman in black was seen again last night."* It sure made a little boy stay in after dark.

In addition to the Meeting grounds, the Quakers owned several acres of pasture immediately behind their cemetery. At one period this pasture was rented to the man who carried the mail from Waterford to Point of Rocks. During the summer, this renter had a routine of taking his horse to the pasture each evening at dusk. To shorten his walk back to town, he would cut across the burying ground.

On one occasion there was an open grave, prepared for a burial the next day. Some of the boys from town thought it a good idea to scare this man as he came through the cemetery. One of them got into the grave with a white sheet draped over him. As the man approached, the boy rose up from the ground, making a weird sound. The postman happened to be carrying the bridle, which had a heavy steel bit. When the apparition suddenly appeared before him, the postman instinctively swung his bridle and yelled, "Get back in your hole you s-- b----!!" The bit made contact with the would-be ghost's head, opening a bloody laceration. Never again did anyone try to scare this man.

The Town Triangle & Big Hill

Long before these episodes, or even the Civil War for that matter, old Mahlon Janney made a gift to the town that we still enjoy. A month before his death in May 1812, Janney transferred some of his land at the foot of the Big Hill to the trustees of the village "for the consideration of $1.00, with a desire to benefit the town of Waterford. To build a market house, jail, or any other public building for ever for the benefit of the said town of Waterford." Today, over 180 years later, the market house is gone, but the tank and jail remain as reminders of the past.

The tank is a large cistern intended originally for fire protection; it also supplied water for houses near the corner. The jail, too, has had its place in the annals of the town. In my youth it had few occupants, usually a drunk or chicken thief. There had been a market house on the land, but it had disappeared well before 1900. This building had offered space for town meetings and elections, as well as being a farmers' market. A blacksmith and wheelwright shop shared the site for many years. A ramp for the latter led into the triangle from Water Street. And not least, the triangle also offered evening entertainment as boys gathered to pitch horseshoes, available from Harvey Parker's blacksmith shop.

Amusing stories have been told about the jail; a couple bear repeating. Bob Densmore[i] related that one Christmas Eve afternoon the town sergeant was inside sweeping the floor and building a fire, preparing for a drunk or two that were sure to celebrate to excess. While the sergeant was inside, some boys, who had waited for their chance, pulled the door shut, locking him in. It was a couple of hours before his cries were heard by a passerby and he was released.

The sergeant may have been Oscar Hanvey (1850-1926), a cigar-smoking man who held the job at one time. Hanvey, in any event, once tried to arrest a law violator who turned on him, got the sergeant's thumb in his mouth, and seriously damaged it by chewing on it. Mr. Hanvey used the usual cure for such injuries by wrapping the damaged digit with a cloth soaked in turpentine. While so bandaged, he tried to light his cigar but set the turpentine rag on fire, seriously singeing that part of the thumb left by the original culprit.

---

[i] Bob Densmore was a son of John S. Densmore of the Loudoun Rangers.

The area we call the Big Hill is actually an extension of Main Street. When the town expanded from the vicinity of the mill, builders first erected a few houses along that street, eventually passed the Corner, and then about 1800 ascended the wooded hill in a development called Janney's New Addition.

At the foot of the hill is the Town Branch, which crosses the extension of Main Street, then flows under the Corner Store, Second Street, and the Tin Shop, before flowing finally into Catoctin Creek. Around 1920 a new bridge was put over the stream at the foot of the hill. Rodney Hough, of the Methodist Hough line of excellent woodworkers, was the builder. Huge round logs were flattened on one side and at the ends of the other where they were laid on stone abutments. Mr. Hough flattened the one side with a broad axe, the only time I had seen one used. He did such a good job of hewing it looked almost like it had been sawed.

As one climbs the hill, the first house on the left is one that James Moore built between 1808 and 1815. During the Civil War it was owned by the family of John W. Gover, but in 1872, in a family dispute, it was sold at auction to Daniel Webster Minor. Web Minor was a black man who had worked with the Loudoun Rangers. He was also the father of Hiram, one of the memorable quartet of singers I mentioned earlier.

Foraging

Annie Minor was Web's wife and, like most Waterford women, she knew how to make the most of what the local land and streams offered. Mr. Emerson James, a former neighbor of hers, recalls that he and some friends once caught an eel in Catoctin Creek. They traded their catch to miller Reed Mays for a "mud turtle" that they gave to Aunt Annie. She knew just how to cook it, and rewarded the boys with a taste of the meat.

I could go on for some time about the way early farmers and villagers lived off the land. Hunting was a major activity, most often for squirrels and other small game. Before my day passenger pigeons were eagerly awaited visitors. They were taken in great numbers every year. They are extinct now of course.

People also foraged regularly for wild fruits, and berries and other edibles. Cherries seem to have been a particular favorite with the locals in the 1800s.

Just up the hill from the Minors' place was a building used by the black community in my youth as their Odd Fellows lodge hall. That fraternal order had quite a dignified and colorful burial service. Wearing purple caps and collars, they marched, accompanying the casket, first to the church and then to the grave.

Edward Dorsey (1769-1849), an early leader of Waterford's Presbyterian community, built this structure around 1820-23 as a woodworking shop. Among his best-selling offerings were caskets, as old estate settlements show.

Later, at the time of the Civil War, master carpenter and builder John Hough owned and used the building for his workshop. Still later the Methodists held Sunday school there until they built a church at the top of the hill in 1877. Finally, after the Odd Fellows, the old building was used as a dwelling. It was torn down in 1948.

A portion of James Moore's lot lay behind this building, facing on Water Street. Mahlon Janney owned it in 1805, but a deed from 1807[46] states the log dwelling on it was in the "occupancy of Billy Respas." It sat on the verge of the original Janney-Hague (Hough) line. This is a short distance from the town spring that could have provided the property with water. Could this have been a Janney structure, and one of the *very* first abodes in the settlement?? I don't intend to start a rumor, but it could be an early site in the village.

Farther up the Big Hill on the right is an old brick house that Edward Dorsey built for himself. The next building was built by Thomas Lacey around 1815—originally as two residences. Isaac Hough, who had bought the original lot from Mahlon Janney in 1801, was a brother-in-law of Robert Braden, one of the area's leading businessmen. Isaac had been a Quaker but was found wanting in 1794 for "frequenting places of diversion."

Between the Dorsey and Hough houses, I dimly recall, were the remnants of a harnessmaker's shop—Mr. John Dick McKinney's, if I am not mistaken.

I was born in the George Schooley house across the street. Just up the hill on that side is a house that belonged to Lloyd Curtis, a brother of Malinda Rucker. Uncle Lloyd had been born a slave on one of the Grubb farms north of town. He was quite a practical artisan. I used to watch him make brooms and cobble shoes.

Two memorable spinsters later lived in that house. Miss Martha smoked a clay pipe. Miss Em (Emma) had a son—but no husband. It was an interesting neighborhood.

LLOYD CURTIS (c.1861-1948).

JOHN DIVINE on Main Street Hill. George Schooley house on right, Odd Fellows hall with belfry in background.

At the top of the hill is a large brick house built by Mahlon Janney. I believe he was living there when he died in 1812. In the mid-19th century, Charles Edwards lived there, one of the village doctors. Since my youth, the "front" door has been moved to the east side of the house, which has been painted white.

MAHLON JANNEY house. Lloyd Curtis house at left.

The Big Hill was a wonderful place for sledding. Under favorable conditions one could speed the length of Main Street from the top of the hill to the mill. Someone stood at the street junction to prevent the coaster from running into a horse-drawn vehicle—and later autos. People were not in a hurry in those days and did not mind waiting for some kid to go flying through the intersection.

On cold nights water from the tank was carried up the hill to be poured on certain tracks to create a solid sheet of ice and a wonderful base for speeding sleds. Residents of the hill often had cleats that buckled on their shoes to prevent slipping as they came down. Of course those folks didn't appreciate our creating ice on the hill.

The Double Decker was a homemade contraption that would carry the steerer and about 8 or 10 boys sitting behind him. It would develop impressive speeds as it rumbled down the icy hill. There were accidents and a few broken bones but only one fatality that I can recall. This was the result of a youngster sliding under a parked car about 25 years ago.

VIEW DOWN MAIN STREET HILL, c. 1862. Pictured are Annie Hough with brother Silas.

Horses were "rough shod" for icy roads. This was done by welding pieces of steel to the toe and heels of the shoe. This gave the blacksmith extra work in bad winters. He had to be a real artisan as the shoe, with additions, must fit the horse's foot. In the 1920s there were three blacksmiths in the town, brothers Fred and H.B. Parker and Tom Corbin.

Sledding and sleigh-riding were popular around Waterford long before my time. Nearly everyone it seems enjoyed dashing through the countryside in a horse-drawn sleigh, slipping smoothly and swiftly over roads famous most of the year for ruts, dust and mud.

Sleigh-riding also offered opportunities for courting that were not lost on the younger set. Then as now, though, youthful exuberance sometimes outran common sense. A few days before Christmas in 1867 one young swain "*took Frances sleighing this evening and the horse ran away, the sleigh upset and threw us out. Played smash generally with the sleigh. Got another team and went on ....*"

The next day he noted ruefully in his diary, "*Thought nobody was hurt by the runaway yesterday. Found out this morning that I could hardly get out of bed. Wonder if Frances is feeling badly from it?...Tonight I can hardly stand alone. Oh, how bad I do feel.*"

But the following day, undaunted, he "*started out early this morning sleighing. Went to Wood's mill, then to blacksmith's shop, then to Waterford...Tonight the sleighing is about broken up, but bells are ringing all around.*"[47]

The Christmas season was normally a joyous time around Waterford, but there were exceptions. The distinction for the worst holiday experience must surely belong to poor Daniel Wine, Jr., son of an old village family. The account book of storekeeper Charles Paxson recorded the chain of events without comment: Mr. Wine was married on Christmas Eve, 1867. The day after Christmas he "cut his throat" and died a week later. We can only speculate about the circumstances.[48]

Cold—Good & Bad

Before modern refrigeration came to Waterford, residents in and around the village relied on spring houses and ice houses to keep food and drink cool during the warm months of the year. Spring houses were not common in the town itself, as there were only a few reliable springs to work with, but many families had an ice house. I can remember at least a couple of dozen, although only a few remain today. One of the best is on the south side of Patrick Street, a well-built stone chamber about 12 feet square and as many feet below ground. A weatherboard shed above keeps the elements out.

Cutting and hauling ice to stock these structures was a regular winter chore. In a hard winter any still body of water would freeze thick enough to provide good blocks of ice. If a broad, slow-moving creek or mill pond was not at hand, some farmers would maintain a small pond just for the purpose.

When the ice was several inches thick and ready to harvest, it would be cut into manageable blocks with special coarse-toothed saws. My father,[i] by the way, invented a set of giant tongs to drag the blocks from the water. The tongs were hitched to the horse traces, and the harder the animal pulled on a chunk, the tighter the device clamped. The blocks were then hauled to the ice houses and laid down with a good layer of straw or sawdust all around as insulation. Emma Myers still recalls cold lemonade in the summer—delicious despite the bits of wet sawdust embedded in the ice.

In warmer parts closer to the coast large quantities of ice were routinely brought in by ship from New England and other points north. Most years, though, Waterford had no shortage of winter to produce all the ice it wanted.

A local farmer recorded with obvious feeling one spell of such zero-degree weather in December 1867: "*Cold all day. Very cold, but thank goodness the wind has stopped blowing...Too cold to think of doing anything. Almost froze by the fire.*"[49]

---

[i] Jacob Elbert "Eb" Divine (1874-1966).

That was not just a figure of speech. On Christmas day in 1848 Mary Reed wandered away from her house south of the village and disappeared. Her neighbors searched high and low, but it was three weeks before David Birdsall came across her frozen body on Mrs. Thurza Rice's place.[50]

January 1912 must hold the local record for bitter cold. At *Clifton*, an old farm just south of town, Leroy Chamberlin's wife Charlton[51] noted in her diary on the 6th that things were freezing in the house and cellar, despite the woodstoves. On the 9th a high wind brought in still colder temperatures, accompanied on the 12th by heavy snow. By the evening of the 13th, the thermometer read 14 degrees below zero, and even heavy covering could not keep the apples in the cellar from freezing. The next morning the mercury stood at minus 25! "*Went to the barns at 5:30 A.M...horses literally covered with frost. Decidedly the coldest weather that has been known here. 30 below in Waterford....*"

The struggle with January continued. On the 16th, "*Very high wind all night and today. Snow drifting badly. Tried to go to milk train [at Paeonian Springs] in morning. Could get only halfway—road completely closed. All the streams frozen, had to cut holes in branch for stock to drink...all stock suffering from cold. 17th...went with [horses] to help open roads. Three teams and about 15 men out. Assisted in cutting through about a half-mile drift...reached Paeonian at noon. Brought back empty [milk] cans.*" There is a lot to be said for central heat, insulation and snow plows.

It was another modern convenience, electricity, that eventually ended the era of the ice house—and changed a lot more besides. Service finally reached Waterford in the 1920s, provided by old Leesburg Power, and one by one families wired their houses.

One of the biggest changes was in lighting. To a village long used to making candles or trimming the wicks and cleaning the sooty chimneys of coal oil lamps, the workings of electricity, and even the new vocabulary, took some getting use to. In one family, the elderly maid, on encountering her first electric lamp, tried to extinguish the light by blowing on the bulb. A more forward-thinking resident couldn't wait to "get the church electrocuted."

Electricity also spelled the end of Waterford's old kerosene street lights. I remember our lamplighters, Edgar James and later old Hector Tecumseh Calhoun Hough—everyone called him "Heck"—pulling a wagon around town with coal oil and materials to clean the lamps. At the end of each day one would make the rounds lighting the lamps, then extinguish them later in the evening.[i]

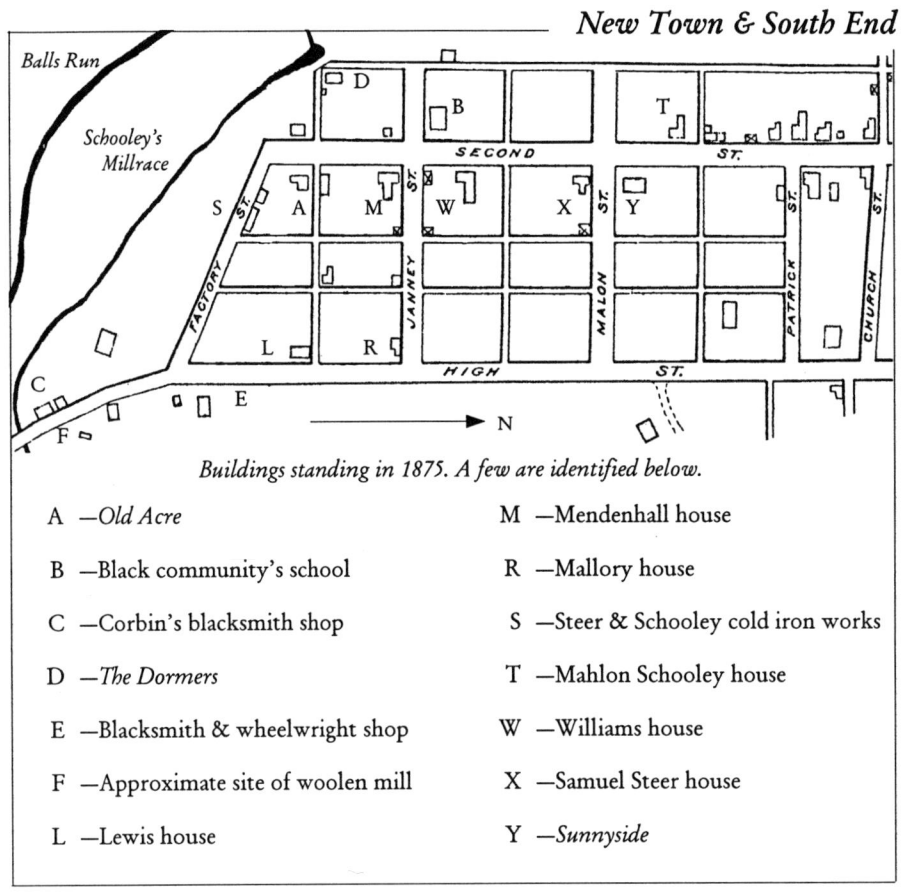

Buildings standing in 1875. A few are identified below.

A —Old Acre

B —Black community's school

C —Corbin's blacksmith shop

D —*The Dormers*

E —Blacksmith & wheelwright shop

F —Approximate site of woolen mill

L —Lewis house

M —Mendenhall house

R —Mallory house

S —Steer & Schooley cold iron works

T —Mahlon Schooley house

W —Williams house

X —Samuel Steer house

Y —*Sunnyside*

---

[i] Edgar Clayton James (1861-1918); H.C.T. Hough (1849-1919).

New Town & the Industrial South End

Not long after settlement moved up the Big Hill toward the Quaker Meetinghouse, an extension branched off Main Street to the south to become Second Street.[i] The lots flanking Second Street came to be called New Town, a name that section kept until well into the 20th century.

It appears that the new street had difficulty deciding whether it would be residential or commercial: it became both. In addition to some fine brick homes, industry appeared at both the north and south ends of the street. Two furniture manufactories and an undertaking shop would grace the north end. At the southern entrance to the village, there was every appearance of a bustling town: two mills, two blacksmith shops, a farm machine manufacturing shop, a slaughterhouse, a school for the village's black children and two private schools for whites. Not all of them operated at the same time, but there was always enough activity to give it the air of a busy village.

No part of Waterford has changed more over the years than that southern part of town, where commercial activity had begun well before New Town was laid out. A resident of the late 19th century would not recognize the area today. Where there was once a busy complex of industrial establishments there are now only residences. It is remarkable how little remains to remind one of those businesses.

The earliest major enterprise in that area was probably a woolen mill that had been built, possibly as early as 1795, on the east side of the road as the village is approached from the south. Not much is known of this mill, which was driven by water from Balls Run. It may have been another venture of miller Mahlon Janney's; he owned all the land involved. In the early 1800s the mill was operated by fellow Quakers James Moore and James Farquhar, both of Irish descent.[ii] In 1815 Moore purchased the property from Janney's estate.

---

[i] First Street was the name given to a short section from the bridge to the mill. It was also called Bridge Street.
[ii] James Moore (c.1757-1826) and James Farquhar (b.1786) both had Irish grandfathers.

The woolen mill or manufactory, as it was known, evidently did a good business. In November 1813 Moore wrote to Lawrence Lewis, a nephew of George Washington, to inform his "*Respected Friend*" that "*the demand for coarse cloths has been so great that we have not made one blanket this season, therefore [it] will not be in our power to supply thee this season but hope before another to be better prepared.*"[52] Perhaps the ongoing war with Great Britain had spurred demand for woolen cloth that year.

In any event the mill apparently operated just 35-40 years. By 1860 Loudoun property records referred to "a brick building formerly used as a mill."[53] Today, only a pit and foundation mark the site.

A quarter of a mile to the northwest, Mahlon Janney built yet another mill around 1803—he was in his early 70s when he embarked on this venture. At about that time he leased—and later sold—to Jonas Potts his original mill at the north end of town.

SCHOOLEY'S MILL

Janney's new operation was a grist and saw mill. Water to drive it came, like that for the woolen mill, from Balls Run. By this time, the original Janney homestead, including an upstream section of the run, had been sold to Joseph Talbott (whose name remains with that farm today). Apparently this transfer of title had no effect on the water supply.[i]

This new mill never manufactured flour, but it provided an additional service over Janney's former mill, grinding hominy and grist (corn meal). It was also a sawmill. I have been told that the sawing was done by the up-and-down motion of a vertically mounted blade until later, when the circular saw became popular. This mill remained water-driven until it ceased operation in 1920. It never had an auxiliary power source such as that installed in the mill at the north end of town.

Mahlon Janney left his newest mill to his nephew Mahlon II in 1812.[ii] Several years later John Schooley purchased the operation, and it has been known as Schooley's Mill since.[iii]

The Dormers, home of John and Milton Schooley

---

[i] Joseph Talbott (1749-1798). Talbott's widow Rebekah later married James Moore, one of the partners in the fulling mill. It was a close community.
[ii] These Mahlons can be confusing! Amos Janney's son Mahlon inherited the mill we know today and later built what we know as the Schooley Mill. Mahlon married Sarah Plummer, but they had no children. Mahlon's sister Mary married her cousin Abel Janney, and they had a son Mahlon, whom I refer to as Mahlon II, rather than "junior."
[iii] John Schooley (1797-1868) left the mill to his son Milton (1833-1908).

Across the Clark's Gap road from the site of the old woolen manufactory, at the corner of that road and Factory Street, is an old stone dwelling that has quite a history.

It appears from the records of the several owners and operators that the place had been built as a blacksmith shop about 1821, probably by Quaker Lewis Coale. Coale had come from Maryland about 1817 and married Phebe Steer in 1820. Sad to say, Phebe perished a year later in the great typhoid epidemic of 1821.

The shop came into the Silas Corbin family in 1868 and remained through two generations of Corbin blacksmiths until the 1940s. In my earliest recollection this building was both a store and blacksmith shop. Thomas Corbin was then the operator, as he had been all of his working life.[i]

Tom Corbin's store was a joy for a little boy to visit as he had just about everything that my small world could envision. Today one might call it a "flea market," as there was much there except for perishables. The blacksmith shop was in the end nearest Balls Run, and there was a two-story section in the north end. The second story was a great place to play if you could sneak by Mr. Corbin and ascend the stairs.

One time a couple of young contemporaries of mine found an old musket up there and not knowing it was loaded carelessly pulled the trigger, shooting a hole through the wood shingle roof. They were lucky to escape before Mr. Corbin arrived at the stairs to block their escape. There was never a clerk in the store, as Mr. Corbin would stop blacksmithing to wait on customers, who were few and far between.

Mr. Corbin was quite an artist in iron, as he made biblical quotations, *e.g.*, *ETERNITY WHERE WILL YOU SPEND IT?* or *PREPARE TO MEET THY GOD*. These items were then hung outside to let the elements "age them," then they were ready for tourists.

About the end of World War II, E.H. Beans bought the shop from the Corbin estate and completely remodeled the stone building into a dwelling and antique shop for his sister.

---

[i] John Thomas Corbin (born c.1860) inherited the business from his father Silas (1832-1905), who had originally inherited it from John Schooley, father of his wife Miriam.

On the north side of Factory Street and east of the house known today as *Old Acre* another enterprise sprang up before the Civil War. James M. Steer, a blacksmith, formed a partnership with his brother-in-law Reuben E. Schooley, a wheelwright, to manufacture and repair farm machinery.[i] Reuben, by the way, was a nephew of the miller, John Schooley, and James Steer was a nephew of Lewis Coale's ill-fated wife Phebe—two more examples of the many tangled relationships that add interest and occasional confusion to Waterford's history.

Steer and Schooley's business thrived. Not only did they repair all types of farm machinery, but they invented a grain drill that became a popular item with wheat farmers. The diagram on the next page best describes the layout of their operation. My grandfather worked there under Reuben Schooley before moving on to a shop on the corner of Factory and High Streets.

OLD ACRE

---

[i] James M. Steer (1810-1874); Reuben E. Schooley (1826-1900).

Grandfather Divine said Mr. Schooley would strictly forbid any smoker to come near his wheelwright shop; he would go into a rage at the sight of cigar or pipe. That is, until the day a representative of Cyrus McCormick came to their shop with the object in mind of purchasing one of their ideas for improving the grain drill. This gentleman not only smoked a cigar but he dropped the ashes into the shavings. Anxious to strike a deal, Mr. Schooley paid no heed to this gross violation of his rule. I have forgotten whether he made the sale.

In addition to these important businesses, there were a handful of residences at the south end of town before the mid-1800s. The Schooleys lived at both ends of Factory Street: Reuben in the brick house near the site of the woolen mill; his Uncle John in a brick house across Second Street from *Old Acre*. And *Old Acre* itself was home to James Steer's father Joseph.

Just to the west of *Old Acre* stood a log house originally used by the miller employed at Janney's new mill. Later, during the Civil War this house was occupied by Mahlon Myers' family. My Uncle Charley Myers was a very young lad at the time, and child-like was fascinated by the soldiers as they passed by his door.

On one occasion young Charley came home proudly wearing a Union soldier's blue coat. Never was a kid happier over a new-found plaything. Then his mother found the reason that the coat had been discarded—it was crawling with body lice. Once the mother came on the scene the coat disappeared in flames and young Charley got the scrubbing of his life in the millrace behind the house.

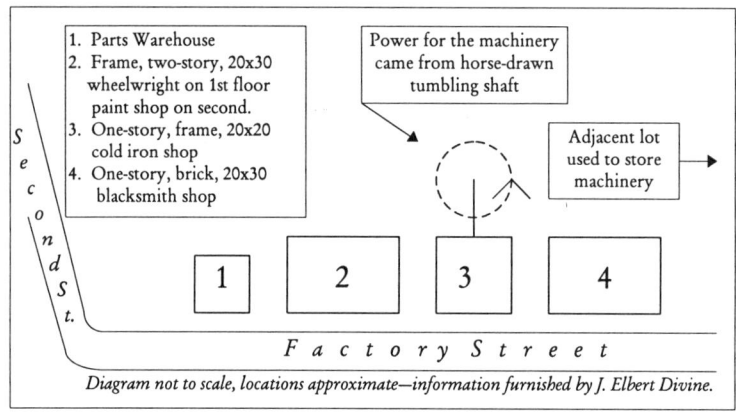

Diagram not to scale, locations approximate—information furnished by J. Elbert Divine.

If we turn now from Factory onto Second Street and head back toward the center of the village, we pass through the New Town development laid out after 1812 by Mahlon Janney's executors. We moderns are most fortunate to have as a guide Miss Rachel Steer, a real link to Waterford's past. Toward the end of her 99 years, in a journal that just came to light in 1996, Miss Steer recounted with great clarity the people and places on Second Street that she knew as a child in 1821.

> Rachel Steer, one of the old Quakers pictured on page 13, was still living in Waterford in 1911, the year I was born. It makes me feel old to think that she had clear memories of William Hough's wife Eleanor Hite, who was born in 1749! She described how "Nelly" in her last years would be carried into the meeting house in an arm chair and set down on a platform between the double doors.

She began her reminiscence of Second Street at *Old Acre*, the home of distant cousins Joseph and James Steer, and proceeded north. I will follow along behind her with a few comments.

"John Lacy lived in the little brick [house] next to James Steer." Mr. Lacy's house is long gone now; it was a haunted-looking ruin to me as a child. Later Raymond "Piggy" Paxson had a small store on the site.

"Then [came the house of] Jacob and [Beulah] Mendenhall where [daughter] Hannah M. Worley afterwards lived and taught school until the Civil War." In my youth, the Mendenhall house had become the Methodist parsonage. Before that it was home to Joseph James and his family. This may have been the same James house that was reported struck by lightning in 1886.

103

Lightening [sic] in Waterford

Last Saturday afternoon the lightning struck the dwelling house of Joseph James in Waterford, causing considerable damage. The electric current tore off one corner of the roof; tore the feet of the rafters nearly all loose from their places; picked up three stoves, which sat in the attic, and threw them five or six feet, damaging two of them; tore up the attic floor and the ceiling of the room below it; cracked and spread out one of the walls (which are of brick); destroyed several doors, nearly all the glass in the house and some of the window sash; and it damaged the plastering so badly that the entire house may have to be re-plastered.

Mrs. James was the only one in the house, but, fortunately, was not injured. A team that was passing was frightened and ran some distance but was controlled by the driver.

—*Loudoun Telephone*, May 21, 1886

HORSE & DRIVER (Hunter Moore) at Second and Janney Streets, near the site of the lightning strike.

The next house was built by John and Lydia Williams *"where [son] William Williams afterwards lived and died. Then came several lots called the commons."* There is still open land south of Patrick Street today, but since Rachel Steer's time several houses have been built along that stretch of Second Street. One of those later houses was once the home of Rachel's brother Samuel Steer, who—like William Williams and Robert Hollingsworth—spent time in a Confederate prison.

> I have often wondered who laid the brick for these several fine homes? Was it Thomas Lacy, William Nettle, or my Great-Great Grandfather Jacob Divine and his brother Bonham? Garrett Hough appeared on the Waterford scene about this time so it is possible that he also may have done some of this work.
>
> I would like to think that Jacob and Bonham Divine did much of the actual construction, as they were tradesmen, not developers as the others were.
>
> Jacob built the Friend's schoolhouse for John Williams, who was treasurer and overseer for Fairfax Meeting.[i] So in 1815-16, when John Williams built his house on Second Street, might he have used the same bricklayer?

WILLIAM WILLIAMS
(1816-1892)

---

[i] I once saw an entry to that effect in an account book of John Williams.

Sunnyside, another "new" house next door, has more Civil War romance connected with it than any other in Waterford.[i] It was built before the war by John B. Dutton, who was prominent in the community as a merchant, insurance agent, member of Friends meeting and father of five, including four lively daughters.

Members of Fairfax Meeting attempted to maintain a neutral position regarding the Union and Virginia's secession, but their sympathies clearly lay with the North and the Confederates evidently saw Dutton and Samuel Steer as too ardent in their support of the Union and drove them out of town. Dutton found asylum across the Potomac in Point of Rocks, Maryland, where he remained during the war, visiting his family only under cover of darkness.

While in exile, he became postmaster at Point of Rocks. This helped the people of Waterford in their struggle to remain in touch with the outside world. Federal postal service had been suspended in seceded states as of June 1, 1861, so citizens of the village improvised by employing independent contractors to carry the mail from Point of Rocks. One of these mail carriers was held up by some of Mosby's men and lost his horse, leaving him stranded in the road with nothing but the wagon. This was Fenton Myers, whose descendants still live in the area.

Upon his return at war's end, Dutton became a Justice of the Peace, to the consternation of former Confederate antagonists. One of those was Capt. Frank Myers, who had been Lt. Col. E.V. White's second in command of the 35th Battalion Virginia Cavalry. When White was elected Sheriff of Loudoun County in 1867, he asked Myers to become his deputy.

Capt. Myers had a parole[ii] as a defeated rebel, but he had never taken the Oath of Allegiance required to hold office. After much foot-dragging, he finally agreed to take the oath, given by the local Justice, who just happened to be John B. Dutton. It would spice up these pages if I were to include here Frank's full diary entry for the day he took the oath, but let's use just one line when he terms Dutton "the lord high priest of the Devil." Dutton left no account of this meeting.

---

[i] For a first-hand account of the remarkable wartime experiences of the Duttons, see Divine, Souders & Souders, *op. cit.*
[ii] Parole: freedom granted by Federal authorities in return for a promise to lay down arms.

This was not the romance that I mentioned, for that involved two of Dutton's vivacious daughters. John William Hutchinson, a soldier with the 13th New York Cavalry, stopped for a drink from Dutton's well, and that sip of water started a courtship resulting in marriage to Dutton's daughter Emma Eliza, known as "Lida," at war's end. Some years ago a great-grandson traveled from California to Waterford to visit the sites and scenes of this early romance. It was a real thrill to see his reaction and excitement as he stood by the well where the original drink of water had been served.

Another daughter, Elizabeth ("Lizzie"), also fell victim to the charms of a Union soldier, Joseph Dunlap, so despite their Meeting's frowning on war, these two Quaker lasses found happiness from the army.

These romances, however, were not the only noteworthy events of this home. In the midst of the war Lida and Lizzie, along with Samuel Steer's daughter Sarah Ann, co-edited *The Waterford News*. This eight-page, brazenly pro-Union newspaper chronicled wartime Waterford with generous helpings of humor. All eight issues, printed by the *Baltimore American*, survive.

SUNNYSIDE. *Shed at left was used at one time to store wool, pending sale to a traveling buyer.*

Turning again up Second Street, we encounter a log house next to *Sunnyside*. It is not a native but was assembled there in recent times from old buildings brought from elsewhere. In Rachel Steer's day the first house beyond the commons was *"John Braden's house built by him."* In 1901 Waterford's growing Loudoun Mutual Fire Insurance Company acquired the location for its new headquarters. Braden's old house was dismantled, but portions of it were incorporated into *Laneslea*, erected on Factory Street near the site of James Steer's old cold iron works. The brick insurance building, in turn, became a residence when the firm moved to its present home on High Street.

Now the family connections get a little complicated again, so bear with me. John Braden (1777-1847) had three daughters, all of whom married sons of Joseph Vandevanter. John also had a brother Robert, mentioned previously as one of Loudoun County's early tycoons. Robert Braden at one time or another owned several houses in the Waterford area. Rachel Steer reminds us that one of Robert's homes was the brick house at the corner of Second and Church Streets *"which Decatur Vandevanter now [1903] owns."* And Decatur was a nephew of John Braden's daughters. I think this is a good time to cross Second Street and resume Rachel Steer's tour on the west side.

"Opposite the vacant lots [the commons mentioned] above, John Livingstone built the house now owned by Virginia H. Mansfield. His wife was Joseph Pierpoint's sister." Actually, Mahlon Schooley—brother of the miller John Schooley—built this fine brick house in 1817, selling it to Livingstone the following year.

Livingstone's wife Elizabeth died amid the typhoid epidemic of 1821 and his fortunes went downhill from there. He suffered financial reverses in 1824 and lost the house. Still unable to discharge his debts, the stricken man "asked" to be dropped from Fairfax Meeting; they obliged him in 1826.

David and Sarah Taylor Mansfield eventually bought the house in 1867. I remember their daughter Virginia, who was quite an artist and still living there when she died in 1920.

Rachel Steer recalled that *"a weaver by trade lived next [door], then a man named Palmer in the white house...."* I do not know about the weaver, but the "white house" is the one now called *Catoctin Creek*, after a school operated there by a 20th-century owner. The original portion may predate New Town itself by a year or two. Mahlon Janney sold the land it was built on to Joseph Talbott, Jr., in 1810.

Talbott was another in the long line of Quakers who did not measure up to the standards of Fairfax Meeting. Before he was 22, he had married contrary to meeting discipline and "joined in light company, frolicking and dancing." The meeting promptly disowned him in 1796. Evidently unrepentant, Mr. Talbott went on to open a tavern on Main Street.

The John Palmer of Miss Steer's memory undertook the first of several additions to the house before Mary Ann Taylor bought it in 1823. Miss Taylor was a sister of Sarah Taylor Mansfield, who lived two doors down, and of Harriet Taylor Steer, just across the street. Unlike most of her educated kin, she was illiterate.

"The large brick [house at the foot of Patrick Street] was built by Samuel Hough for his mother Lydia."[i] This would have been about 1819. Word has it that Samuel ran afoul of Fairfax Meeting for marrying "out of unity" and left town not long after. He sold the house to his mother for $3,500, a huge price at the time. I prefer to think that this was a measure of its unusually high level of workmanship and detail, rather than filial price-gouging.

"Next came the William Nettle house which he built, then Isaac and Susan Walker's."

I have mentioned Mr. Nettle earlier as Waterford's first mayor. He made a name for himself as one of the town's master builders, and he may have had a hand in building the Samuel Hough house next door.

In his later years Nettle (1779-1856) was a trustee of the local Baptist congregation. Curiously though, he and his wife Sarah (Sallie) are buried in the Quaker cemetery.

The Walkers next door were prominent Quakers. Isaac was Jacob Mendenhall's partner in a dry goods store on Main Street. Susan Talbott Walker was a half-sister to back-sliding Joseph, Jr., but she and each of her own four surviving children stayed faithful to Fairfax Meeting, married well and prospered. One wed William Williams; another—J. Edward Walker—married twice, the second time at age 80 to Sarah Ann

---

[i] Lydia Hollingsworth Hough (b. 1752), widowed daughter-in-law of Old John Hough.

Steer, Samuel and Harriet's daughter. (Regrettably, that proved too much for him—he died a few months later.)

Rachel Steer does not address the final two houses on the west side of Second Street, other than to mention that the woman living in the first was "*Mary Shawen, David Shawen's mother*...." I believe she was the widow of Cornelius Shawen, one of the directors of the old Loudoun Company.

RACHEL STEER said William Nettle built this house. Others believe it is the work of Israel Griffith. It is often called the Doctors' House, after several later occupants.

I propose now to leave the 1820s and look at Second Street a century later, in my childhood. To me at that time the commercial activities were the most interesting.

Across Second Street from the Corner Store is a low brick building that was built in 1872 by the Loudoun Mutual Fire Insurance Company. By the early 1900s, the insurance company had moved to its new quarters down at the corner of Patrick Street and the older building became a meat shop managed by E.L. James.[i] Mr. James and son Minor operated this business for thirty years.

```
E. L. JAMES
DEALER IN
FRESH MEATS
```

Their butcher was Mr. Frank Rinker,[ii] a man who enjoyed a good laugh, usually at a small boy's expense. He would sit in front of the building in a chair, propped against a tree, calmly chewing his cud of tobacco. He would flip a coin, usually a penny, up in the tree and pretend he was shaking money from it. When he drew several boys to pick up the money, he would spit tobacco juice on bare feet. His hearty laugh could be heard all around that corner of town.

The meat shop did a big business in fish (Potomac River herring) in the spring of the year. Farmers bought huge amounts of fish to salt down in barrels. Salt herring was the standard breakfast food for farm families and their hired help. I have been told that my grandfather would buy 6,000 fish each spring, a large enough quantity that they cost less than one cent each.

---

[i] Ernest Linwood James (1864-1947).
[ii] Edward Franklin Rinker (1853-1924).

At Thanksgiving and Christmas, the meat shop handled oysters. The only time I ever ate oysters was at those two dates; at $6.00 per gallon, they were a real delicacy. Orders were placed about ten days in advance and they were received a day or two before the holiday. The gallon cans, packed in ice, were shipped up on the railroad to Paeonian Springs. Later, when Minor James got a Model T truck, he would drive to the wharf in Washington, D.C., to get them.

Each Saturday in the summer months Mr. Rinker ran a horse-drawn meat wagon from Waterford to Hillsboro. I went with him to open farm gates and received fifty cents a day for my labors—don't laugh, it bought a lot.

The frame building above the Town Branch next door came to be called the Tin Shop. E.B. Myers[i] and son Leslie were the tinners (roofers) for a large area, not restricted entirely to Waterford. Expert workmen, they came along in a transitional period when the early wood roofing shingles needed replacing and the asphalt shingles we know today had not appeared.

THE TIN SHOP

---

[i] Edward Bruce Myers (1865-1941)

Mr. Myers had grown too old to climb in the time I remember him, so his son Leslie did the roofing, and Mr. Myers tended to the metal work at the shop. He was quite adept with a soldering iron, repairing housewives' pots and pans, as well as soldering lengths of guttering and downspouting to save Leslie time on the job. Today you would go to K-Mart for a cup; in those days, Mr. Myers would make you one.

He was also an avid follower of the "Amos 'n Andy" radio show. Mr. Myers would come to the corner store to loaf, but at five minutes to seven you would see him head for home.

While on the subject of rural artisans, I remember Mr. Ed Myers had a brother Robert, an excellent plumber. Mr. Bob would always draw a crowd at the evening loafing sessions because of his ability to tell funny stories. The story is told on him that he installed a water system for a rural family that included putting in a concrete tank, or catch basin. He, being a better plumber than concrete worker, created a horrible monstrosity. So he scratched into the wet concrete, "Not much for looks, but Hell for strong."

Leslie Myers was also the town recorder in the latter years of Waterford's incorporation, which ended in 1936.

At one point this building was owned by Mr. William Bennett,[i] who leased part of it to the post office. From 1885 to 1889 he himself was the town postmaster, and for a time my Aunt Clara was assistant postmaster there. The most memorable event of that period was a severe thunderstorm that caused the Town Branch to rise, washing out some of the supports of the post office floor. The floor collapsed, dropping a safe and Aunt Clara into the torrent. The safe sank, but she managed to crawl out about 100 feet downstream.

---

[i] William T. Bennett (1833-1896).

HORSEPOWER

The building beside the Tin Shop was used as a livery stable. Anyone who missed seeing this enterprise in action missed an important part of growing up: the horses, the hayloft, the corn cribs, the watering troughs, and everything it took to operate a horse-drawn taxi service were all there near the center of town. Buggies and carriages for hire, teams for heavy hauling and garden plowing—the livery stable had the answer for every need.

The clientele was both local and from outside. Salesmen would ride the train to Paeonian Springs and then rent a horse and buggy from Waterford to work small stores in outlying places.

There was also a carry-all—a two-horse conveyance that the Waterford band and baseball teams used. The African-American families of the village hired the same vehicle every September 22 to take themselves to the Emancipation Day celebrations in Purcellville. Sarah Gordon remembered riding in it about 1904.

Every stable had at least one attendant besides the owner. He was kept busy feeding and grooming horses, checking teams in and out, and caring for the vehicles.

Ed Beans was the owner/operator in my time and I have heard him tell the story several times of a horse he had named Old John. There was a distillery over at Burkittsville, Maryland, that sold *Golden Gate* whiskey. I don't know whether that brand was any better, or whether it was more convenient to get, but it seemed to be popular with the Waterford drinkers.

Mr. Beans said that Old John was regularly in demand to make the trip to Maryland because he could always bring the intoxicated driver home. Many times, when he went at early dawn to open the stable, the horse would be standing there, waiting to go in. His passenger was passed out, dead to the world, but Old John had brought him safely home. Maybe it would be good if we had a few Old Johns now. At least there would be fewer D.U.I.s.

That is not to say that transportation by horse was always safe. Waterford's history is full of stories of people who came to grief around these powerful animals. Sometimes, just as today, we can blame "driver error." And in those days, too, the young were often the ones who got into trouble.

Civil War diarist Rebecca Williams sympathetically noted the suffering of nine-year-old Anna Dutton, whose jaw was broken when a horse kicked her in 1862. Burr Paxson tersely recorded the death in 1889 of African-American Fill [sic] Webster—"killed by James Walker's colt." And Paxson's nephew Charles broke his neck in a fall from his horse—no seat belts in those days. I could go on.

The risks did nothing to dampen local enthusiasm for horses, though. Whether for work or pleasure they were as essential then as the tractor and automobile are today. In 1868 Isaac Hoge reported to the Catoctin Farmers Club on some fine Percherons fresh from France that he had seen exhibited at the Frederick County [Maryland] fair. He judged these big work horses *"very superior, of fine size and action"*—a lot of horsepower was not just an expression in those days.

EDGAR HOUGH BEANS and wife Margaret. Ed, son of Amos Beans, ran the livery stable in what was later the public garage; he also bought horses at the "Red Barn" behind it.

The previous August Waterford had staged a horse show of its own, generating some local excitement. Frank Myers, the young fellow whose horse smashed his sleigh, was one eager attendee: *"Plowed fast all forenoon so that I could finish...and go to the...show. Col. White [his old Confederate cavalry commander] came to dinner and then I went to Waterford with him. Saw some fine horses working gaily without bridle lines or harness."*[54]

Young Myers was, in fact, a keen judge of horses good and bad. His understandable favorite, though, was his old cavalry charger, converted after the war to farm use. On August 2, 1865, he wrote in his diary that *"poor old Black Hawk [was] very sick all day. I cried over him but it didn't do any good. Then I sent for Mr. Hope and he cured him."*

Valuable animals were always a temptation to some, and after the Civil War, especially, horse thievery was a real problem. The situation was complicated by the fine line during the war between stealing and requisitioning animals for military purposes. In December 1862, for example, the aforementioned Lt. Col. White—then a major—was obliged to authorize Waterford Quaker James M. Walker *"to take from any of my command his bay mare, light made and a dark bay horse blind in one eye, the said bay mare & horse were taken from their stable on the night of the 13th Dec. 1862, and supposed to be taken by some of the stragglers of my command."*[55]

The problem persisted after the war, forcing establishment in the county of a Citizens Organization for the Recovery of the Stolen Horses—many in the Waterford area were members.

One who was involved on the other side of the matter was Ed Wright, a young miller who had enjoyed a checkered career with White's command and who evidently had some difficulty adjusting to the South's defeat and his return to civilian life. In October 1865 Myers noted in his diary rumors *"that Charles and James Cooper are stealing horses. If they are I know Ed Wright is engaged in it and is making tools of the Cooper boys."* Candor obliges me to mention that my Great-Aunt Mary was married to Wright for a time.[i]

---

[i] Mary Alvernon Divine (1841-1931).

Even after automobiles became plentiful, horses remained important in Waterford, especially in the winter. The unpaved roads around would be cut up so badly with farm wagons and wet weather that many people would put their cars away about the first of December and rely on horses to get them around until spring. You could buy your yearly license tags on April 1, instead of January when they were due, and save one quarter of the fee. A lot of people did that.

> Cars were garaged; horses needed shelter as well. I can remember three sheds for their protection against the weather while owners were at church or school. All of these were of the same design: a sloping roof, closed in on three sides with the open side to the south, sheltered from the north wind. Each had about the same number of stalls or divisions—ten or twelve as I recall.
>
> One of these sheds was at the Baptist Church. It stood on the north side of the lot, running along Church Street, with the open side facing the church. There was another at the school house (now the Old School), running along and facing Fairfax Street. The third was at the Friends Meeting. The northwest corner of this last one was about where the stone plaque now stands. The shed ran toward the Meetinghouse and opened south toward the cemetery.
>
> I don't know the financial arrangements for the two church sheds, but with the school, each stall belonged to an individual. The family had paid for the construction, and they in turn sold the stall to another when their child/children finished school. As late as 1929 a few stalls were still being used for buggies or horseback riders.

Mr. Francis Peacock tells another story of the days when horses and automobiles shared the roads near Waterford. It seems that the townspeople had finally arranged for the paving of Clark's Gap Road, their main link to the outside world. All went well until Edgar Peacock, grandfather of Francis, found them paving the stretch through his farm. He insisted that *"that new road is too hard for my old mare Lark,"* and demanded that they tear up the offending section. They did.

Waterford's livery stable was the scene of the village's only known murder, if we don't count the wartime bushwhacking of William Grubb in 1861 and a couple of other deaths attributed mysteriously to "foul play."

Warren O'Haira, a veteran of the Spanish-American War, had moved to Waterford after his army service because his girlfriend lived there. On the evening of July 24, 1900, a summer thunderstorm had driven several people into the livery stable, where an argument arose between O'Haira and Ernest Mullen (not related to my mother's family) over O'Haira's girl friend. Apparently the argument grew heated and Mullen, in fear, picked up a club and struck O'Haira a blow on the head that proved fatal.

Mullen ran but was captured and held overnight in the store building at the west end of the Graham House. He was guarded by men appointed by Decatur Vandevanter, the Justice of the Peace. That was one occasion when Waterford's old street lamps burned all night.

Mullen was taken to Leesburg the next day. At his trial, he received a sentence of only seven or eight years and was back in the county within a few years. O'Haira was buried in the Waterford Union Cemetery with a government grave marker commemorating his military service.

A Village of Veterans

Men of Waterford, a village founded on principles of peace, have been involved in virtually every conflict since the birth of the Republic—even before, if you count "Old John" Hough, whose horses were impressed for use by the Fairfax militia during the French and Indian Wars.[56]

The Revolutionary War put the Quakers in a tough position. Several, including Old John's son William, put patriotism above the strict pacifism of their meeting to join the Continental Army. Fairfax Meeting promptly expelled many (but not all) of those, including Francis Hague, Jr., for their decision to fight. Men who refused service, on the other hand, risked a stiff fine from the revolutionary government.

Garrett Hough was one of the veterans of the War of 1812. A master builder who had come to Loudoun from Maryland, he was the progenitor of a long line of Methodist Houghs around Waterford. His son George served in the Mexican War in the 1840s.

The Civil War, of course, embroiled many Waterford men on both sides, including a number of African Americans who fought for the Union. Many local boys died; others were maimed, like "Cripple Bob" Hough, old Garrett's grandson.

Simon Elliott Chamberlin, a New York cavalry officer, liked what he saw of the Waterford area during that war—including Edith Matthews, the local girl he met and married. Their sons Edward and Leroy were among the first to begin the restoration of Waterford's crumbling buildings.

After the war and his marriage, by the way, Capt. Chamberlin served briefly with the 8th Cavalry in the wild West—in Washington Territory.

Sons of Waterford have also fought in the wars of the 20th century. But that is another story.

At the southwest corner of the livery stable, a lane ran down to the Red Barn and slaughterhouse. The barn was built for overflow of horses from the livery stable, and the slaughterhouse was used by James Meat Market. As a kid I worked for Minor James and Mr. Rinker (still for fifty cents a day) while they butchered. I carried water and was a real "gofer." I can still remember the sting of the salt in nicks and cuts as I worked the preservative into fresh, slippery hides with my bare feet.

One summer, hornets had built a nest under the eaves. Said nest was shown due respect by all of us country people. One time though, while we were butchering, a couple of city boys came in to watch. Not content just to observe the work, they also prodded the nest with a stick. Mr. Rinker warned them twice to leave it alone. Soon we heard a loud wail and one of them grabbed his head. When he could talk, he said, "That animal bit me right back of the ear! Come on, let's get out of here!" Mr. Rinker gave forth with great laughter, and, needless to say, we had no more boys that day.

At the foot of the same lane ran the millrace, which figured in another story. There was a certain gentleman in town who never worked and was supported only by his sisters. As he put it, *"I was born on Saturday, after all the work was done."* He always dressed well and strutted around, acquiring the name The Senator. He went too far though when he took undue liberties with a local girl. Several boys took corrective measures by throwing him in the millrace. Of course, no one admitted to doing it, but the next day, a crude sign, with an arrow pointing toward the race, hung on the livery stable reading, **The Senator's Private Bathing Beach.**

Such ill-advised encounters between the sexes were too common then as now. But in those days retribution was more often swift. On one occasion, when word got around that a local man had compromised the virtue of a young lady of the town, Waterford boys again took it on themselves to right the wrong. As the offender returned home one night, they pelted him with rotten eggs. Thereafter he was known, at least to the boys snickering in private, as Eggs Walker.

The present Waterford Market was built as such by Mr. Flavius Beans. Flave operated the store until age caught up with him—he was born about 1848. Then his wife Rosa boarded school teachers in the apartment above or fed visitors on a per meal basis. Rosa in her later years was a very stout woman. She would sit in a rocker in the window of the store there and keep up with the world on Second Street.

In 1921, Waterford had a baseball team in the County League, which allowed each team a certain number of outside players. The Waterford team imported several from Frederick, Maryland, and before home games they were fed lunch at Mrs. Beans' boarding house. We little boys would stand in awe to watch these imports file in and out of her dining room. By that date the store had closed, so she used that area as a dining room when she fed extras. As I look back, Waterford developed some equally good teams with all home-grown talent—and we didn't get $5 or $6 per game plus a meal.

Rosa Beans was the daughter of Waterford's well-known chair manufacturer and mortician Lewis N. Hough. She and her sisters Elizabeth, Ella and Carrie share their own part of the town's history.

I have mentioned that Rosa's sister Elizabeth (Miss Lizzie) Hough married E.C. James and ran a boarding house of her own on Main Street. And Ella was the Hough sister who married L.P. Smith, long-time churchman, merchant at the corner store and undertaker at the building on Second Street where he carried on the work of his father-in-law.

Third sister Carrie Hough married Decatur H. Vandevanter, who, like his brother-in-law Lem Smith, was an undertaker as well as a farmer and Justice of the Peace. Together these four ladies carried on an important part in the community by their good works, in keeping with their Hough ancestry.

The chair manufactories of Lewis Hough and John Mount were both on the east side of Second Street. Chairs from one or the other once graced every dining table in the village. These days the Waterford chair has gained much prestige. If you doubt it, go to a public sale when one is offered.

Mount's factory has long since gone, but Hough's survived as an undertaker's building. The town council met upstairs, a space also used for a time as the local lodge of Fraternal Americans. Still later the building saw simultaneous use as a gas station, barber shop, and hardware store, the name we know it by today.

THE OLD DOMINION
SPLINT BOTTOM
Hickory Chair.

I PRESENT this Loudoun made Chair to the public, which for Comfort, Strength, Neatness and Durability, we challenge the trade to equal it. The best material used in their MANUFACTURE, and the most skillful workmanship used in their MAKE. I will sell as cheap as can be bought in the county, full satisfaction guaranteed, call and examine and decide for yourselves at my FACTORY, in WATERFORD, Loudoun county, Va.

☞ All orders promptly filled and Chairs well packed and delivered free of any extra charge on the cars or at any point on the river.

Undertaking
A SPECIALTY.

I am also prepared as usual to furnish any thing in this line of business that may be called for. I keep on hand the very best WALNUT CASKETS and BURIAL CASES, with French Glass Tops, and can fill any order at the very shortest notice at moderate prices and no extra charge for distance. I also manufacture the plain Walnut, Cherry and Mahogony Coffins when desired. Thankful for past favors L. N. HOUGH,
nov 1-tf   Chair Factory, Waterford, Va.

Church Life

Waterford has always been a mostly god-fearing town, from the pious Quakers to the Presbyterians, Baptists, Methodists, and others who followed them. It would be hard to exaggerate the role of the churches in both the spiritual and social life of the village. Here, though, I will leave the theology to others and instead try to convey some of the lighter moments of these worthy organizations.

From earliest days the congregations tended to put their churches on high ground, geographically as well as spiritually. Three—Presbyterian, Baptist and Methodist—still stand on High Street.

The old Presbyterian manse was built in 1884 adjacent to the church. The Baptist congregation always shared their minister with another church, and he lived out of the village.

The Methodist parsonage was at the corner of Janney and Second Streets. The Waterford Methodist Church was part of a six-church circuit and was limited to two Sunday evening services a month. That schedule was arranged so that the minister did not have to commute home after the evening meeting.

All three churches shared in a Wednesday evening prayer meeting, and all three had Sunday School picnics. The reward for going to Sunday School was two-fold: the picnic, when ice cream flowed abundantly, and the Christmas program, when we got an orange and a small box of chocolate drops.

The Christmas program also gave all of us amateur actors a chance to perform. Any similarity between our Three Wise Men and the real Magi was purely coincidental. Only the parents appreciated that group of squirmy little boys singing *Away in a Manger* off key.

The picnic woods were on Talbott Farm at the top of Trough Hill (off what is now Route 704); later, when autos were more plentiful, we went to an amusement park at Braddock Heights, Maryland, where there were sliding boards and merry-go-rounds.

CHURCH PICNICKERS *fording Balls Run*

One year, a very energetic Methodist minister came to town and organized an Epworth League. While this was basically a Methodist organization, all three churches joined in. Attendance was good, as there was not much else for youngsters to do on Sunday evenings. In addition to those Sunday sessions we frequently had socials on Friday nights during the summer. A requirement of the roll call was that each must answer with a verse from the *Bible*; John 11:35 really took a beating from those too lazy to do their homework.

Aunt Dolly lived at the top of the Big Hill across the street from the Methodist Church; in summer she could hear the entire service from her front porch. One hot summer evening a deacon from the church came over to borrow a pitcher of water. Thinking it was for the use of the minister, Aunt Dolly put a big chunk of ice in it. The next sound heard was a loud wail from the child who had been christened with the ice water.

Another summer years earlier, as I have mentioned, there had been a more serious episode at the neighboring Baptist Church. After the battle of August 27, 1862, the sanctuary was so badly damaged that it was fourteen years, 1876, before it was repaired and the congregation ready to resume worship service.[57]

Five years after the walls were rebuilt the congregation was blessed with a dynamic young minister, the Rev. Charles T. Herndon. Stories of his ministry in Waterford are legendary. He soon knew everyone in the community whether they were members of his church or not. He was a friend to all, and he visited often around the entire area.

A story is told that he was friendly with, and often called on, Millard Janney, a Quaker who ran the mill at Wheatland.[i] One of these visits came in mid-summer during a serious drought. As Rev. Herndon was leaving, Mr. Janney said, "*Charley, you Baptists are great for prayer. How about praying for rain so I can start grinding again?*" A few days later came a violent thunderstorm. The flood of water washed out Janney's mill dam, causing him to send word to Rev. Herndon that, "*I'll never ask a Baptist to pray for me again, they always overdo it.*"

This kind of banter was typical of the more or less friendly rivalries among the various church denominations in Waterford. I guess it was Nicholas Cresswell, the dyed-in-the-wool Anglican, who got things off to a good start with his characterization of his Quaker hosts as practicing "a stupid religion indeed." He was similarly gracious about followers of other non-Anglican churches, describing them as dupes of "*religious quacks...and fag-end-of-the-Scripture mongers.*"

Waterford's Friends gave as good as they got, and they tended to be fussier than some about those they admitted to the fold. Lyle Beach,[ii] for example, was a hard-working cooper of modest means who once expressed interest in joining Fairfax Meeting. I have heard that someone from the Meeting told the crestfallen Beach in so many words, "*We believe we have all the members we need, right now.*" There is a happy ending, however. Mr. Beach is taking his eternal rest at the Fairfax burial ground—perhaps his Quaker wife interceded on his behalf.

As for the Methodists, a report from Pastor W.H. Wilson in 1880 urged great effort to support the Sunday School in Waterford lest its members be "captured by the Presbyterians."

My own Grandfather Divine, a Methodist who had not seen that much of the world, attended a funeral high mass for his twin sister in 1931, she having married and become a Catholic. On leaving the service,

---

[i] Millard Fillmore Janney (1857-1920).
[ii] Lial/Lyle Beach (1813-1884).

which was held in Washington, D.C., the old man commented crustily that he didn't see much difference between it and sun-worshipping.

There weren't many Catholics around Waterford in the old days. Those that there were had to be ministered to from afar—in the mid-1800s one local family, at least, was served by a priest from Harpers Ferry.

There were fewer Jews than Catholics. Shortly after the Civil War though, young Meyer Greenebaum[i] moved to Waterford with his wife and children and opened a store. He did considerable business with another storekeeper in the village, Charles E. Paxson (1818-1903). Paxson's account book for the years 1866 to 1870 shows a clear progression in his regard for Greenebaum as he got to know him. In the first year Paxson's entries referred guardedly to "the Jew," as in *"paid Jew for 1 sack coarse salt."* As the newcomer won his trust, however, "Jew" disappeared entirely, and after experimenting with many variations Mr. Paxson even learned to spell Greenebaum's name correctly—well, almost correctly.

Aside from the churches, I have said little about the upper side of town. With a few exceptions like the Meeting House and Mahlon Janney's last home, this area was developed more recently than much of the village. The name Butchers Row probably dates from the mid-19th century. Edwin Atlee, a livestock dealer and justice of the peace, owned land on both sides of that short stretch of road, including the site of the future Old School. In 1870 he was buying slaughterhouse fixtures.

Two or three old houses in that area have disappeared. One burned in the 1960s; another, Henry Virts' old house across High Street from the Baptist Church, was torn down many years ago to make way for a larger residence. My father helped build the replacement.

---

[i] Meyer Greenebaum came from Germany, where he was born about 1842.

SCHOOL DAYS

The history of education in Waterford began long before the Commonwealth of Virginia established free schools in 1871. Although taverns outnumbered schools four to two in the village in 1830, the Quakers, at least, had always been mindful of the importance of a good education for their children. And in providing for their own they did not exclude those of other faiths from their schools.

Several buildings still standing in the village once housed Quaker schools. The oldest is the small brick building at the rear of the Meeting House. It was used as a school as early as the late 18th or early 19th centuries. When this structure was enlarged and remodeled as a dwelling in the mid-20th century, blackboards were found painted on the walls.

There were also early schools in private homes—and merchants to provide educational supplies. An estate inventory of Samuel Pierpoint's store on Main Street in 1813 included, along with chocolate and casket hinges, "*3 testaments at 30 cents each, 15 primmers [sic] at four cents each, and four spelling books at 17 cents each.*"

In the 1850s Miss Mary Ratcliffe (1827-1907) operated a school in her mother's house near the tanyard on Main Street—Pierpoint's old house. Hannah Mendenhall Worley's school on Second Street was probably in operation even earlier. And next door to Mrs. Worley, William Williams established before the Civil War a school for his and other children in the small brick dependency on his property, according to descendants.

During the war young Elisha Walker (b. 1844) taught in a small brick schoolhouse (near the intersection of Clark's Gap and Trough Roads) built by his father James Walker on the family farm. Finally, at the turn of the century, Elisha's brother Robert established near his house on High Street a school for his daughter Cornelia and other young ladies of the area. My Aunt Agnes Mullen was one of those.

The Quakers also worked closely with the Freedman's Bureau and the local black community immediately after the Civil War to found Waterford's first school for African Americans. Reuben Schooley sold a lot on Second Street for the new building, and Miss Sarah Ann Steer taught the first students—some of them adults. That old school operated for almost a century, educating some fine citizens. It closed finally in

1957 but is again in use today as part of a living history program, bringing the past to life for new generations of students.

STUDENTS *at school on Second Street, c.1920, with their teacher, Mr. Winston Walker*

The frame building—now a residence—just to the north of that Second Street school was constructed as yet another Odd Fellows lodge, but it also served early in this century as an industrial school, where black children of the area learned practical arts such as home economics. Sarah Gordon was one such student.

The first public school for white children was built around 1878 on the site bounded by High Street and Butchers Row. This three-room, seven-grade school was called the Waterford Academy. My father was among the first students.

The Academy building came to an untimely end. In February 1909, the janitor left a bucket of hot ashes on the wooden floor after cleaning the coal stoves. The school burned to the ground.

Private donations, insurance, and money from the Literary Fund, I am told, paid for a new building on the old site; the new Waterford School opened in time for the 1910-11 term. Meanwhile classes had been held in the basement of the Baptist Church.

The Waterford Academy

With few exceptions, Waterford School was blessed with good teachers. They certainly were not in it for the money—salaries in 1904-05 were just $27 per month.

It is always dangerous to rate or even name teachers, lest some fine ones be overlooked. I will nonetheless mention two who made a great impression on me.

My first grade teacher, Miss Mary Shawen[i] led her pupils gently from freedom to the discipline of academic life. Miss Minnie Russell,[ii] who lived on Patrick Street, was a great mathematician for the 6th and 7th graders. Miss Minnie taught at least two generations of students—the parents of some of my classmates had studied under her.

---

[i] The Shawens are an old Waterford family. In 1815 Cornelius Shawen was one of 12 directors of the Loudoun Company, the county's first bank. Miss Mary (1858-1925), who lived at *Old Acre*, was descended from those early residents. Her sister Frances (Fanny) married Waterford's Frank Myers of "Lige" White's 35th Battalion—but only after keeping the hardened cavalry officer in uncertain torment for several years.

[ii] The Russells have also been prominent around Waterford for many years. Miss Minnie (1868-1942) lived in town with her unmarried sisters Ida (1859-1928) and Edmonia (1870-1945). Edmonia was postmistress for 25 years.

Miss Minnie was a stern task-master with but one aim: make every student ready for the next grade. I can picture her with her starched white apron and high black collar standing in front of a class after we had not performed to her standards in a quiz. *"Well! I'm ashamed of you! But I promise you, you will learn this work or we will still be on these pages at the end of the school term!"* These were not idle words, for you did learn it as you were afraid not to respond. A great regret of mine is that on her death I could not stand at her grave and say, *"Thank you, Miss Minnie."* A World War II date with Uncle Sam had taken me away from Waterford.

From the heartland of America came a Hoosier schoolteacher, Winifriede Elliott, who made contributions to the social, as well as academic, life of the village. "Frieda" married in Loudoun, forsaking her native Indiana to become a true Waterfordian in every sense of the word.

The name Frieda Myers became synonymous with education at the high school level, church work, and with the broader family life of the community. She became principal of the high school for a term and a half, after Mr. Vivian Ayers resigned midterm in 1926. She brought with her a discipline that the school had not previously known; of this, the writer of these lines has first-hand knowledge. Never again did a 16-pound shot, used in track, ever fall down the ventilator duct, nearly shaking every window loose.

Not that Mrs. Myers lacked a sense of humor. She told a story that captured life in Waterford at Christmas time, when friendliness reigned supreme: Mrs. Myers had a near neighbor and, in the custom of the time, she invited this neighbor in to visit and sample her fruit cake. This fine lady had but one fault: occasionally she would speak without thinking. On that day, as they ate the fruit cake, Mrs. Myers remarked thoughtfully as she tasted it, *"I think it needs a bit more spice...."* Whereupon the guest replied, *"Most anything that was done to it would have helped!"*

For a school so few in numbers, we had good athletic teams—girls basketball, men's baseball, and mixed tennis. In 1925, we won the county baseball championship, defeating Round Hill 4-3 in a real thriller for the title. One of the great days in our young lives was the following Monday morning, when at assembly, the principal, Mr. Ayers, made a speech of congratulation.

Mr. Ayers, by the way, was courting a teacher that year who boarded with Mrs. Flave Beans in the rooms over the present Waterford Market. There were two large buckeye trees in front of the building, and Mr. Ayers would park with the bumper of his new Durant auto against one of them when calling on his lady friend.

One night some boys wired his bumper to the tree and hid nearby to see what would happen. Mr. Ayers finally came out and started the car, which immediately choked out when he tried to back away. The next attempt he applied a little more gas, with the same result. The third time he applied enough gas to make his wheels spin. This brought him out of the car and revealed the reason for his troubles.

Not until well into the 1930s was there county school bus transportation. Some of our students came by horseback, some by horse and buggy, and maybe a couple by auto. But the greatest number came on foot. It was a sight to see the twenty or more pupils forming a group to walk out the road to Paeonian Springs at the end of the school day.

One evening, as this cavalcade went out the Paeonian road, a boy somewhat on the sissy side said to another, *"Don't get too close to me, you have bugs in your head."* (Head lice were a common pest, afflicting those whose mothers didn't scout them often.) The accused replied, *"I'll put a bug in your head!"* and threw a stone, hitting his accuser in the intended target and opening a wound that needed treatment.

The school auditorium, as I mentioned, was built in 1928 and was a long-awaited addition to the institution. The graduating class of that year (two in number) was the first to inaugurate the new facility, and what a struggle it had been to ready it for the occasion.

Two ladies of the community should forever be enshrined in the history of this building. In 1927-28 Mrs. Josephine Carr and my mother Nannie Mullen Divine worked tirelessly to raise money for a curtain, two stoves and chairs. These items were not included in any appropriation made by the School Board.

These ladies produced plays and organized any event that would raise a few dollars. The curtain cost $400, maybe not so much money today, but a large sum in 1928. Stoves were not important that spring or summer, so they could wait. Chairs were salvaged from Paxson's Hall, those that were not broken down.

I do not remember anything of note in that first event, but the class of 1929 (my class) had an embarrassing moment during the baccalaureate sermon, which was delivered by the minister of Madison Parish. With no air conditioning, all windows were opened and a stiff breeze blew the preacher's notes away. After shuffling his remaining papers for a few minutes, he mumbled, "*Oh, well,*" and jumped ahead a few unrelated paragraphs to continue his sermon. Not many people thought it made much sense anyway.

The graduation of the three-member class of 1930 had its own modest excitement. When Emma Myers, valedictorian and daughter of Josephine Carr, rose to give her valedictory address, one of the old "collapsible" chairs from Paxson's Hall failed again, throwing the front-row occupant into the aisle. Only the usual laughter that followed these occurrences gave the startled Emma the respite needed to collect her thoughts and start her speech.

Emma tells me that one of the plays produced to raise money was "Safety First," which never won any Oscars or Emmys but was so successful that it was produced in Ashburn, Hamilton, and Bluemont after its run at home.

The Community League, grandfather of the PTA, was the vehicle the ladies used to raise money to finish the auditorium. To those not familiar with this parent organization, it was really a citizens' association, but most of its energy was directed toward the school. Its monthly meetings, in addition to a business agenda, included a program put on by pupils. I made my stage debut there with a recitation of John Greenleaf Whittier's *The Barefoot Boy*.

A story grew out of Mrs. Carr's hectic efforts to equip that building and the several meetings of the League. Her husband, James W. Carr, and his brother Ernest, worked on the old Smith farm east of Waterford, but Ernest never married and always made his home on Second Street with brother James and his wife. One night, Mrs. Carr was late for a meeting of the League, and someone said, "*I wonder where Mrs. Carr is?*"

Young Van Davis Hudson, the precocious eight-year-old son of the Methodist minister had the answer: "*I think one of her husbands is sick.*"

The two large Victorian frame houses on the east side of High Street south of the Old School were built around the turn of the century. Robert Walker, son of James Walker of Talbott Farm (Amos Janney's old homestead), built the house on the right for himself, enlarging Charles Hollingsworth's old residence. The other he built for his unmarried sister Edith. Miss Eed, as we called her, always dressed formally in a black silk dress and high collar.

Beyond the old Presbyterian manse on the south corner of High and Janney Streets was a house that burned many years ago. It was the home of African Americans Charlie and Mary Mallory. Mary could read and write, and I remember that she would write letters for older members of the black community who did not know how to.

PRESBYTERIAN CHURCH *and old manse*

The house just to the south of the Mallory's once belonged to my Grandfather Divine. I believe it was built by a black man, James Lewis, about 1850 when he purchased the lot for $75. I think this Lewis was a relative of the James Lewis who served with the 55th Massachusetts during the Civil War. Frank and Mollie Steer—the oldest of John B. Dutton's daughters—bought it just after the war in 1865, then sold it to my grandfather in 1875. I lived for a time there with him and Aunt Clara in the 1930s.

JAMES LEWIS HOUSE

Back at the industrial end of town, on the east side of High Street where it meets Factory, were a blacksmith shop and wheelwright shop. In my time Fred Parker was the blacksmith, following his brother and father at that shop.

The wheelwright shop was run by my grandfather, Joseph Divine, who had learned the trade from Reuben Schooley. This was the same Reuben Schooley who was a partner in the manufacturing firm of Steer and Schooley. Grandfather was serving his apprenticeship when he went into the Union Army; after the war he continued to work until the age of eighty-three. Being a good Methodist, he never drank or smoked, but he loved a steady diet of cold mutton, which to me was solid fat. However, cholesterol had not been invented, so he survived the large doses to age 91.

Fred Parker continued to run the blacksmith shop until the property was sold to Mr. Charles Elliott, a retiree from Indiana. Mr. Elliott had retired in Waterford because daughters Frieda and Eleanor had preceded him there and married local men, Douglas Myers and Howard James.

On a rainy day during the summer months this shop and the one operated by Mr. Parker's brother near the Corner Store downtown were swamped with horses waiting to be shod. This was the busy season for the farmers, and rainy days were the only ones they could spare from their crops. Literally from morn to dark horses were lined up awaiting their turn for new shoes or tightening of worn ones.

Immediately upon purchasing this piece of property, Mr. Elliott started to work. First he moved the blacksmith shop up nearer the dwelling for storage. This he did by laying down poles and forcing the building along inches at a time. Next he tackled the two-story wheelwright shop by dismantling it board by board. He used the framing to enlarge the blacksmith shop and the weatherboarding to build a fence across the front of the property. To make his pickets or palings he sawed the old siding lengthwise, *by hand*.

I mention this because Mr. Elliott attacked this project in the spirit of early Waterfordians who built things with their own hands. I would stop by to see him work and chat with him to ask questions about his project. Overwhelmed with his ambitious work plans, I once said to him, "Mr. Elliott, this is going to take a long time." His reply was, *"John, I hope I never finish."* He never did.

Nor did John Divine, but he would not have had it any other way. For all that he did contribute, Waterford is forever in his debt.

POSTSCRIPT

After World War II, John Divine and other returning veterans found that the town had undergone many changes in four years. Several people he had known since childhood had died, but the greatest surprise was the large number of newcomers. He was a virtual stranger in the town where he had grown up, no longer able to greet by name everyone he met.

Postwar housing shortages in the Washington area had driven wartime workers to the outer suburbs, including Waterford. While some of the new arrivals did not stay long, others adopted the town and stayed on to the benefit of the community. One of the latter, in John's view, was Allen B. McDaniel, who had come to the village in the late 1930s:

This may be one man's opinion, but Allen McDaniel did as much to bring recognition to the town as anyone since the Janneys established a mill and town on the banks of Catoctin Creek. He had made the Friends' Meetinghouse into a dwelling without disturbing the exterior. In 1943 he enlisted the aid of several local citizens to organize the Waterford Foundation for the revival and promotion of arts and crafts.

Since its founding, Waterford had been a self-subsisting area. With fertile land and plenty of water power, all the valley of the south fork of Catoctin Creek needed was an industrious, innovative people. These artisans came, and before long Waterford required very little from the outside for daily living. These skills Mr. McDaniel wanted to recall from the past, and soon he found many with like feelings. Those who thought Mr. McDaniel's idea was only a pipe dream should visit Waterford early each October.

A lady who had moved here from New England told me this story: She went back home to visit friends. One asked her where she was then living. Thinking that no one there had heard of Waterford, she replied, "Near Leesburg, Virginia." Her friend asked, "Is that anywhere near Waterford?"

The little mill town had gone national.

NOTES

1. *Walk With Us: A Walking Tour of Waterford*, Waterford Foundation, 1992.
2. Photograph courtesy of Taylor Chamberlin, Waterford, Virginia.
3. Rankins' remarks are taken from a 1967 manuscript, in the author's collection, on Methodists in Waterford by Melvin Lee Steadman, Jr., of the Virginia Methodist Historical Society. Steadman cites an original document in the Garrett Institute.
4. John T. Phillips II. *The Historians Guide to Loudoun County, Virginia*. Goose Creek Productions, Leesburg & Middleburg, Virginia, 1996, p. 207.
5. Nicholas Cresswell. *The Journal of Nicholas Cresswell 1774-1777*, Kennikat Press, Inc., Washington, N.Y., 1968, p. 138.
6. *Ibid.*, p. 163.
7. William Wade Hinshaw. *Encyclopedia of American Quaker Genealogy Vol. VI*, Ann Arbor, Michigan, Edwarde Brothers, Inc., 1950 (reprinted 1994); Marty Hiatt, *Early Church Records of Loudoun County, Virginia*, Family Line Publications, Westminster, Maryland, 1995, pp. 111, 115; Phillips, p. 456.
8. Mill structure described in policy N2116 issued to lessee Jonas Potts by Mutual Assurance Society in 1803.
9. Loudoun County Deed Book C-Part One, pp. 367-369, June 15, 1762.
10. Briscoe Goodhart, Co. A, *History of the Independent Loudoun Virginia Rangers, 1862-65*, McGill & Wallace, Washington, D.C., 1896, p. 24.
11. Loudoun County Will Book B, pp. 355-356.
12. *Ibid.*, pp. 387-388, (inventory of the estate of Francis Hague).
13. Phillips, pp. 213, 223-232, 282, 296.
14. Means does not appear in the records of Fairfax Meeting. His parents were birthright Quakers of Campbell County, Virginia, and he was born into the meeting. When he married Quaker Rachel Bond in 1856, however, she was noted as having "married out of unity." [William Wade Hinshaw, p. 472.]
15. *Ibid.*, p. 536.
16. *Ibid.*, p. 472.
17. "Records of Free Negroes," Certificates No. 1615, 1617, Loudoun County Circuit Court.
18. Hiatt, p. 136 (Minutes of Fairfax Meeting, 1st Month, 1785).
19. Hinshaw, p. 511.
20. From papers of E.M. Chamberlin, Jr., courtesy of Taylor Chamberlin.
21. Loudoun County Court Order Book D, 1767-70, p. 161, March 14, 1769.
22. Emerson James provided these recollections. He is a grandson of Edgar and Elizabeth James.
23. Loudoun County Circuit Court records: Coroner's Inquests.
24. Helen Hirst Marsh, "The Loudoun Company," *Bulletin of the Historical Society of Loudoun County*, 1962, pp 43-48, Potomac Press, Leesburg, Virginia, 1962, republished 1997, Historical Society of Loudoun County, Goose Creek Productions, Leesburg & Middleburg, Virginia.
25. Loudoun County Will Book 3F342, March 20, 1888.

26. Walter Fred letter to Eugenia Smith, May 23, 1883, in collection of co-authors.
27. Reminiscences of Rachel Steer (1814-1912).
28. Orson Blair Curtis, *History of 24th Michigan of the Iron Brigade*, Detroit, 1891.
29. Loudoun County Will Book D, pp. 341-343.
30. Hinshaw, p. 501.
31. Loudoun County Will Book O, pp. 424-426.
32. *Loudoun Chronicle*, August 15, 1849.
33. Virginia Acts of Assembly 1817-1818, pp. 181-182.
34. Joseph Martin, *Gazetteer of Virginia and the District of Columbia*, Charlottesville, 1835, p. 216.
35. Deposition of Noble S. Braden in Loudoun County Chancery suit (folder M140), April 14, 1836.
36. Commonplace book of Mary Frances Dutton Steer.
37. 1850 manuscript census, U.S. Census of Waterford.
38. Goodhart, p. 38, Goodhart was a participant in the battle.
39. *Ibid.*, pp. 35-36.
40. E.M. Chamberlin, Jr., from Taylor Chamberlin.
41. Goodhart, pp. 127-128.
42. *Ibid.*, p. 118.
43. Letter of Joseph T. Divine, November 1, 1863.
44. Goodhart, pp. 179-180.
45. Franklin M. Myers, unpublished diary, entry for March 19, 1867.
46. Loudoun County Deed Book 2I221.
47. Myers, entry for December 19, 1867.
48. Account book of Charles E. Paxson, 1866-70. Transcription in Waterford Foundation Local History Collection.
49. Myers, entry for December 14, 1867.
50. Loudoun County Coroner's Inquest, January 16, 1849.
51. Charlton Chamberlin, unpublished diary, courtesy Ann C. C. S. Smith. Transcript in Waterford Foundation Local History Collection. Entries for January 1912.
52. Letter from James Moore to Lawrence Lewis, November 1813.
53. Loudoun County Deed Book 5V304.
54. Myers, entry for August 31, 1867.
55. John E. Divine, *35th Battalion Virginia Cavalry*, H.E. Howard, Inc., Lynchburg, Virginia, 1985, p. 19.
56. Phillips, p. 77.
57. For further reading on this engagement see Franklin M. Myers, *The Comanches*; Briscoe Goodhart's *The History of the Independent Loudoun Virginia Rangers*; and Divine, Souders & Souders, *"To Talk Is Treason."*

BIBLIOGRAPHY

<u>Books</u>

Cresswell, Nicholas. *The Journal of Nicholas Cresswell, 1774-1777.* Washington, D.C., New York, Kennikat Press, Inc., 1968.

Divine, John E. *35th Battalion Virginia Cavalry.* Lynchburg, Virginia, H.E. Howard, Inc., 1985.

Divine, John E.; Souders, Bronwen C.; Souders, John M. *"To Talk Is Treason."* Waterford, Virginia, Waterford Foundation, 1996.

Goodhart, Briscoe, *History of the Independent Loudoun Virginia Rangers, 1862-65.* Washington, D.C.,. McGill & Wallace, 1896.

Hiatt, Marty. *Early Church Records of Loudoun County, Virginia, 1745-1800.* Westminster, Maryland, Family Line Publications, 1995.

Hinshaw, William W. *Encyclopedia of American Quaker Genealogy, Vol. VI.* Ann Arbor, Michigan: Edwarde Brothers, Inc., 1950 & 1994.

Janney, Werner; Janney, Asa Moore. *Ye Meetg Hous Smal.* Lincoln, Virginia, 1980, 1994.

Jewell, Aurelia M. *Loudoun County, Virginia, Marriage Records to 1881.* Berryville, Virginia, Virginia Book Company, 1975.

Jewell, Mrs. Walter Towner (Aurelia). *Loudoun County Virginia Marriage Bonds, 1762-1850.* Berryville, Virginia, Chesapeake Book Company, 1962.

Loudoun County Historical Society, *et al. Bulletin of the Historical Society of Loudoun County 1962.* Leesburg, Va., Potomac Press, 1962.

Martin, Joseph. *Gazetteer of Virginia and the District of Columbia.* Charlottesville, Virginia, Mosely & Thompkins, Printers, 1835.

Myers, D.N. and Taylor, H.B. *The Mutual Fire Insurance Company of Loudoun County, Virginia, 1849-1949.* Waterford, Virginia, 1949.

Myers, Franklin McIntosh. *The Comanches.* Baltimore, Maryland, Kelly Piet & Co, 1871.

Phillips, John T., II. *The Historian's Guide to Loudoun County Virginia, Vol. I, Colonial Laws of Virginia and County Court Orders 1757-1766.* Leesburg, Virginia, Goose Creek Productions, 1996.

<u>Articles, Pamphlets and Newspapers</u>

Spellman, Sheri and Souders, Bronwen C. *Walk With Us: A Walking Tour of Waterford.* Waterford Foundation, Waterford, Virginia, 1992.

Steadman, Melvin Lee Jr. "Methodists in Waterford." Virginia Methodist Historical Society, 1967.

Genius of Liberty (Leesburg) 1818-1821.
The Loudoun Telephone (Hamilton) 1878-1901.
The Loudoun Chronicle (Leesburg) 1846-1851.
Loudoun Telegraph, a/o 1888.

Public Records, Manuscripts and Unpublished Works

Leesburg, Virginia, Loudoun County Circuit Court and T. Balch Library:
    deed and will books, "Records of Free Negroes." Coroners inquests and chancery records at court only.

Leesburg, Virginia, collection of author:
    working notes of land ownership and families in Loudoun County and predecessor counties Prince William and Fairfax.
    Diaries of Franklin McIntosh Meyers, 1865, 1867.
    Copy of Letter from James Moore to Lawrence Lewis.
    Letter of Joseph T. Divine, November 1, 1863.

Waterford, Virginia, Waterford Foundation Local History Collection:
    Policies of Mutual Assurance Society and Virginia Acts of Assembly, 1817-1818.
    Chamberlin, Rose Charlton: *Farm diary 1910-1914,* transcription.
    Federal Census manuscript records, 1810-1920 for Waterford, Loudoun County, Virginia.
    Paxson, Charles E. *Account book, 1866-1870,* transcription.
    Steer, Mary Frances Dutton, *Commonplace Book.*

Photographs and Maps

Local History Collection of the Waterford Foundation, Inc., including Historic American Building Survey photographs on pages 22 & 57, unless otherwise noted.

Collection of the author: Front cover, pp. 9, 10, 77, 83, 84, 134.

Peggy Chalmers Coleman Pancoast: pp. 22, 46, 61, 73.

John Middleton: 128.

Taylor M. Chamberlin: 13.

Back Cover: Loudoun Times-Mirror, Leesburg, Va., Douglas Graham.

Map of Waterford from James Oden Survey, 1875, drawn for Charles Phillips Janney of Leesburg, 1875.

R. Jones & K. Littlefield. *Virginia Obsolete Paper Money.* Virginia Numismatic Association, Annandale, Virginia, 1992. With permission.

Thanks to descendants of Waterford families who have visited/shared their research: *Braden, Caldwell, Carr, Collins, Cleggett, Cross, Curtis, Dean, Dulin, Dutton, James, Graham, Gray, Griffith, Hague, Hollingsworth, Hough, Hutchinson, James, , Kenady, Lacey, Janney, Mallory, Minor, Mitchell, Moore, Myers, Oxley, Paxson, Phillips, Pierpoint, Potts, Robinson, Rucker, Russell, Schooley, Shawen, Shuey, Steer, Stephens, Timbers, Vandeventer, Walker, Williams, Wine.*

INDEX

1st U.S. Colored Troops Infantry, 39
6th Virginia Cavalry, 43
13th New York Cavalry, 107
24th Michigan Infantry, 55
35th Battalion Virginia Cavalry, 68
55th Massachusetts Regiment, 134

—A—

Abby Ann (slave), 47
African Americans, 8, 9, 32, 38, 39, 119, 127, 133
alcohol, 11, 28, 60, 71, 87, 114
Anderson, Capt. Charles F., 84
Anderson, Sgt. Fleming, 84
Andrews, John, 28
Anglican Church, 17, 18, 28
Anti-Saloon League, 60
apples, 95
apprentices, 41
Arch House, 62
Atlee, Edwin A., 126
auditorium, 131, 132
automobiles, 49, 51, 117
Averill, Richard, 14
Ayers, Edward, 9
Ayers, Vivian, 130, 131

—B—

Back Street, 32
Ball, Henry, 44
Ball, John, 18
Ball, Stephen, 27
Balls Run, 19, 23, 97, 99
Baltimore American, 59, 107
bank, 48
Bank House, 48
Baptist Church, 79, 84, 117, 128
Baptists, 8, 28, 109
barber shop, Heber Schooley's, 68
baseball, 121, 130
baseball teams, 114
basketball, 130
Beach, Lial/Lyle, 125
Beans, Edgar H., 24, 100, 114, 115
Beans, Flavius, 121
Beans, Rosa Hough, 121, 131
Beatty, Sgt. James H., 83
Belt, Campbell, 44
Bennett, William T., 113
Bentley, Wade, 51
Big Hill, 29, 88, 92, 97
bilious fever, 27
Birdsall, David, 95
black school, 40
blacksmith, 93, 101
blacksmith & wheelwright shop, 87
blacksmith shop, 25, 97, 100, 134, 135
Blue Ridge Mountains, 12
Bond family, 27, 35
Bond Street, 10, 32, 35
Bond Street meadow, 25
Bond, Ann, 35
Bond, Asa Moore, 25, 35, 64
Bond, Dr. Thomas, 35
Bond, Edward, 35, 64
Bond, Elizabeth Moore, 35
Bond, Joseph, 25, 35
Bond, Joseph, Jr., 35
border collie, 24
Boyd, Jennie, 34
Braden, John, 64, 108
Braden, Noble S., 49, 66
Braden, Robert, 66, 89, 108
bricks, 69, 105
brickyards, 69
Bridge Street, 97
broad axe, 88
Brown family, 27
Brown, H.C., 44
Brown, Joseph, 32
Brown, Lilly Hough, 55
Bucks County, Pennsylvania, 14
Burkittsville, Maryland, 114
Buster, 2
butchering, 120
Butchers Row, 126

—C—

cabinet-making shop, 54
Caldwell, Joseph, 38
Caldwell, Samuel B.T., 44, 49
Camelot School, 48
Cameron Parish, 28
canal, 21
canoeing, 46
Carr, Ernest, 132
Carr, James W., 132
Carr, Josephine, 131, 132
Carr, Peter, 28
carriage painter, 53
caskets, 89
Cassady, William H., 50, 59
Castle Thunder Prison, 44
Catalpa Grove, 47
Catholics, 126
Catoctin Creek, 12, 14, 15, 17, 19, 23, 65, 88, 108
Catoctin Farmers Club, 11, 115
Catoctin Mountains, 12
cattle, 23
Cavins, William, 28
Cemetery, Fairfax Meeting, 86
chair and coffin manufacturer, 75
chair manufactories, 121

Chamberlin, Charlton, 95
Chamberlin, Col. Simon Elliott, 85, 119
Chamberlin, Edith Dawson Matthews, 40, 85
Chamberlin, Edward M., 85, 119
Chamberlin, Edward M., Jr., 48
Chamberlin, Eleanor (Bide), 85
Chamberlin, Justin, 85
Chamberlin, Leroy, 85, 119
Chamberlin, Paul, 85
Chamberlin, Taylor, 3
Charles II, King, 8
cherries, 54, 88
Children's Day, 36
Christmas, 76, 93, 112, 123
Church of England, 28
Church Street, 117
Church, Baptist, 123
Church, Methodist, 124
Church, Presbyterian, 123
churches, 123
Chute, The, 23
cider, 21
cider mill, 21
Citizens Organization for the Recovery of the Stolen Horses, 116
Civil War, 32, 43, 44, 45, 59
Clapham, Henry, 21
Clark's Gap, 85
Clark's Gap road, 28, 85, 117
Cleggett, Caroline/Clementine, 37
Clendenin, Mary Chamberlin, 25
Clendenin, William, 25
Clifton, 85, 95
Coale, Lewis, 64, 100
Coale, Phebe Steer, 100
Coates, Clarence, 51

cobbler, 59
cock fights, 64
Cocke, Catesby, 14
Coghlin, Edward, 64
cold, 94
College of New Jersey, 28
Collins, Edward, 57
Collins, Leeford, 58
Collins, Marietta Timbers, 57
commons, the, 105
Community League, 132
Confederacy, 45
Confederates, 43, 44, 45, 106
Connard, Jane, 38
Cooksey, Obediah, 27
Cooper, Charles, 116
Cooper, James, 116
Corbin, John Thomas, 93, 100
Corbin, Miriam Schooley, 100
Corbin, Silas, 100
Corby Hall, 42
corn cobs, 21
Corner Store, 75, 77
Cost, Jonathan, 64
Craven, Alfred, 74
Cresswell, Nicholas, 17, 125
Curtis, Lloyd, 89

—D—

David, Jenkins, 28
Davis, Mary Virginia Hough, 55
Davis, Oscar, 55
Dean, Adolphus Fuller, 37, 56
Dean, George Washington, 37, 38, 56
Dean, Mary Elizabeth Cleggett, 37
death, 34
Densmore, Bob, 87
Densmore, John S., 87
Divine, Bernice "Mac", 3
Divine, Bonham, 105

Divine, Charles William, 39, 51, 59
Divine, Clara, 77, 78, 113, 134
Divine, Cressford, 51
Divine, Elizabeth Dodd, 10
Divine, Frances Bogue, 18
Divine, Jacob, 10, 36, 105
Divine, Jacob Elbert (Eb), 72, 94
Divine, Joseph T., 77, 84, 101, 125, 134
Divine, Mary Alvernon, 116
Divine, Nannie Mullen, 131
Divine, Sarah (Sally) Ann Roberts, 56
Dorsey, Edward, 89
Double Decker, 92
Douglass, Capt. William, 16, 28
Dr. Well's Wonder Herb Cure, 71
Dunlap, Joseph, 107
Durant, 131
Dutton, Anna Ellen, 115
Dutton, Elizabeth, 107
Dutton, Emma Eliza (Lida), 107
Dutton, John B., 53, 106

—E—

Earlham College, 81
Edmonds, Sanford, 54
education. *See* schools
Edwards, Charles, 91
eel, 88
Eggs Walker, 120
electricity, 95
elevator, 21
Elliott, Winifriede (Frieda), 130. *See* Myers, Winifriede
Elliott, Charles, 135
Emancipation Day, 114
England, 14
epidemics, 27
Epworth League, 124

Evergreen Lodge 51 (I.O.O.F.), 60

—F—

Factory Street, 100
Fairfax County, 17
Fairfax Meeting, 17, 18, 38, 60, 81, 86, 105, 106, 119, 125
Fairfax Meeting House, 136
Fairfax militia, 119
Fairfax Street, 117
Fairfax, Lord, 14
farm machine manufacturing shop, 97
Farquhar, James, 97
Ferrell, Annie, 36
First Street, 97
fornication, 18
Fort Delaware, 44
Fort Pillow, Tennessee, massacre, 58
Fraternal Americans, 121
Fred, Annie Smith, 50
Fred, Eugenia (Ginnie) Smith, 50
Fred, Frank, 50
Frederick, Maryland, 16, 121
free blacks, 38
Freedman's Bureau, 127
French and Indian Wars, 119
Friends Literary Society of Waterford, 66
Friends Meeting House, 117
Friends Temperance Union, 60
fruit cake, 130
fulling, 34
furniture manufactories, 97

—G—

Gaskins, Edward, 36, 42
Gaskins, Judy, 36
Gaskins, Moses, 36

George (slave), 47
George Schooley house, 78, 89
German Settlement, 12
Germans, 12
Germany, 73
Gettysburg, 55, 77, 78
ghosts, 85, 86
Golden Gate whiskey, 114
Goodhart, Briscoe, 83
Goose Creek, 12, 59
Gordon, Sarah Rucker, 21, 32, 74, 114, 128
Gover family, 45
Gover, Ann T., 13
Gover, Henry T., 49
Gover, Jesse, 45
Gover, John W., 88
Gover, Margaret Parkins, 45
Gover, Miriam Taylor, 45, 82
Gover, Samuel, 45
Gover, Samuel A., 40, 45
Gover, Sarah Janney Harris, 45
Gover, Temperance Matthews, 45
Grace (slave), 47
graduation, 132
Graham house, 52, 118
Graham, Bob, 53
Graham, Tamar McGavack, 47
grain drill, 102
gramophone, 46
Grandma Reed, 53
Great Depression, 23
Greenebaum, Meyer, 126
Griffith, Israel Thompson, 27, 64
Griffith, James, 63
grist, 99
Grubb farms, 90
Grubb, William, 43
Guinea Bridge, 59
Gwynedd Meeting, 27

—H—

Hague, Francis, 15, 18, 19, 20, 28, 30, 31
Hague, Francis, Jr., 18, 119
Hague, Jane Yardley, 15
Hague, Mary, 18
Hague, Thomas, 28
Hague-Hough house, 31, 33
Hammer, Charles, 73
Hanson (slave), 47
Hanvey, Oscar, 87
harnessmaker's shop, 89
Harpers Ferry, West Virginia, 84, 126
Harris, Samuel, 64
Healer of Waterford, 35
Helen (slave), 39
Henson (slave), 39
Herndon, Rev. Charles T., 125
herring, 111
High Street, 29
Hillsboro, 112
Hillside, 32, 33
Hinshaw, William Wade, 36
Hirst, J. Terry, 69
Hoge, Isaac, 115
Hollingsworth, Abigail Parkins, 44
Hollingsworth, Charles, 133
Hollingsworth, Lewis, 44
Hollingsworth, Rachel Stone, 44
Hollingsworth, Robert Isaac, 44
hominy, 99
Hopewell Meeting, 27
Hopkins, Caroline (Carrie) James, 46
Hopkins, Clarence, 46
hornets, 120
horse hospital, 72
horse sheds, 117
horse show, 116
horse stealing, 116

horses, 21, 26, 39, 43, 52, 93, 94, 95, 114, 115, 117, 119, 131, 135
Hough family, 27
Hough, Clarice, 55
Hough, Eleanor Hite (Nelly), 103
Hough, Ella, 75
Hough, Garrett, 105, 119
Hough, George, 119
Hough, Hector Tecumseh Calhoun (Heck), 96, 128
Hough, Isaac, 89
Hough, Isaac Steer, Jr., 55
Hough, John, 31, 89
Hough, Joseph, 25
Hough, Lewis Neal, 66, 75, 121
Hough, Lydia Hollingsworth, 53, 109
Hough, Mary, 38
Hough, Old John, 119
Hough, Robert B., 73
Hough, Robert W. (Cripple Bob), 77, 78, 119
Hough, Rodney, 88
Hough, Samuel, 109
Hough, William, 25, 31, 74, 103, 119
Hudson, Van Davis, 132
Hunterdon County, West Jersey, 15
Hutchison, John William, 107
Hutchison, Louisa, 3

—I—

ice, 94
ice cream parlor, 73
ice houses, 94, 95
infrared photography, 25
Ireland, 48
iron storage house, 62

—J—

jail, 87

James Meat Market, 120
James Moore house, 88
James, Edgar Clayton, 45, 96
James, Eleanor Elliott, 135
James, Elizabeth (Lizzie) Hough, 45
James, Emerson, 3, 88
James, Ernest Linwood, 34, 111
James, Howard, 135
James, Joseph, 104
James, Minor, 111, 112, 120
Janney's Mill, 19, 20, 25, 35, 55
Janney's New Addition, 88
Janney Street, 123
Janney, Abel, 16, 99
Janney, Amos, 14, 17, 19, 20, 33
Janney, David, 27
Janney, Elizabeth, 27
Janney, Joseph, 16, 17, 28, 35, 56
Janney, Mahlon, 20, 28, 29, 34, 40, 87, 89, 91, 97, 98
Janney, Mahlon, II, 99
Janney, Mary, 99
Janney, Mary Yardley, 14
Janney, Millard Fillmore, 125
Janney, Moses, 64, 66
Janney, Samuel M., 59
Janney, Sarah Baker, 16
Janney, Sarah Plummer, 99
Janney-Hague (Hough) line, 89
Jews, 126
John Braden's house, 108
John Brown's Lane, 32
John Wesley Methodist Episcopal Church, 36
Jones, Hannah, 16
Joseph Janney/George Dean house, 56

—K—

Kelly, Mr., 72
Kent, Dan, 25, 57
Kingwood, 15
Kitty Leggett house, 55

—L—

Lacey, Thomas, 89, 105
Lacy, John, 103
lamplighters, 96
Lane, William, 38, 73
Laneslea, 108
Laura Page house, 50
Leesburg Power, 95
Leggett, Kitty, 56
Lemon, Bill, 59
Lewis, Gladys Jackson, 3, 34
Lewis, James, 134
Lewis, Lawrence, 97
lice, 102, 131
Liggett Street, 25
Liggett, Catherine (Kitty) Rinker Wright, 55
lightning, 104
Lincoln, 59
Literary Fund, 128
livery stable, 114, 118
Livingstone, Elizabeth, 108
Livingstone, John, 108
Lodge, The, 45
Loudoun Cavalry, 43
Loudoun Company, 48, 62, 129
Loudoun County, 17, 28
Loudoun County High School, 25, 57
Loudoun Mutual Fire Insurance Company, 32, 45, 49, 108, 111
Loudoun Rangers, 35, 39, 52, 53, 70, 79, 83, 84, 87, 88
Loudoun Telegraph, 11
Loudoun Telephone, 104
Loudoun Valley, 12, 17, 19
Love, E.N., Dr., 51

Loyal Citizens of Loudoun County, 44
Luckett, Samuel C., 49
Lutherans, 28

—M—

Mahlon Janney house, 2, 91
Mahlon Janney/Asa Moore/Sam Means house, 34
Main Street, 25, 28, 54, 55, 88, 97
Mallory, Charlie, 133
Mallory, Henrietta (Ret), 32
Mallory, Mary, 133
Mallory, Paul (Scoopum), 51
Mallory, Tom, 32, 33
Man on the White Horse, 85
Mansfield, David, 108
Mansfield, Sarah Taylor, 108, 109
Mansfield, Virginia, 108
Market House, 64, 66, 87
Market Street, 64
Matthews, Edith Dawson Matthews, 119
Matthews, Edward Y., 40
Matthews, Mary (Marie) Ruth, 40, 68
Matthews, Sarah Gover, 40
mayor, 35, 64
Mays, Reed, 88
McCormick, Cyrus, 102
McDaniel, Allen B., 136
McDonald, Duncan, 40
McGavack family, 47
McGavack, Andrew, 47
McGavack, Israel, 47
McGavack, John Thomas, 45
McGavack, Lewis, 47
McGavack, Patrick, 47
McGavack, Patrick, Jr., 47
McGavack, Pleasant, 47
McGavack, William, 47
McGeach, Joseph, 38
McIlhaney, John, 28
McKinney, John William (John Dick), 49, 89
McNulty, Hugh, 48
Mead, John, 14, 15
Means, Rachel Bond, 35
Means, Samuel C., 21, 35, 39, 43, 79
meat shop, 111, 112
medicine shows, 70, 71
meetinghouse, 18
Mendenhall house, 104
Mendenhall, Beulah, 104
Mendenhall, Jacob, 52, 104
Merchant, Landon, 85
Methodist Church, 89, 123
Methodist parsonage, 123
Methodists, 8, 16, 28, 88, 89, 104, 119, 124, 125
Mexican War, 119
midwife, 74
milk train, 95
mill, 19, 20, 21, 23, 35, 69, 97, 98
Mill End, 31, 32
mill race, 23, 49
mill storage house, 33
mill, woolen, 97
miller, 21, 23
millrace, 120
mills, fulling, 34, 97
Milltown, 21
Minor, Annie Clapham, 88
Minor, Daniel Webster, 88
Minor, Hiram, 51, 88
Minor, Nathan, 40, 74
Mock, Jacob, 39
Moore family, 27
Moore, Asa, 34, 35, 60
Moore, Elizabeth, 35
Moore, James, 27, 35, 63, 89, 97
Moore, John, Dr., 53
Moore, Thomas, 35
Moore, Thomas, Jr., 35
Mosby, John S., 83, 106
Mount, John, 38, 64, 121
mud turtle, 88
Mullen, Agnes, 127
Mullen, Ernest, 118
Mullen, Florence Virginia (Dolly), 77, 85, 124
murder, 118
mutton, 134
Myers, Capt. Franklin M., 106, 116, 129
Myers, Charles, 102
Myers, Douglas N., 66, 135
Myers, Edward Bruce, 112, 113
Myers, Emma Carr Gentry, 3, 94, 132
Myers, Fenton, 106
Myers, Frances Ann (Fanny) Shawen, 129
Myers, Frieda, 130. See Myers, Winifriede (Frieda) Elliott
Myers, Jonathan, 15
Myers, Leslie, 112, 113
Myers, Mahlon, 102
Myers, Mary, 15
Myers, Robert, 113
Myers, William, 15
Myers, Winifriede (Frieda) Elliott, 135

—N—

National Historic Landmark, 9
Native Americans, 12, 37
Nettle, Sarah (Sally), 52, 109
Nettle, William, 52, 64, 66, 105, 109
New Town, 47
Newcomer, Emanuel, 31
Nichols, Joseph, 59
Northern Neck, 8

—O—

O'Haira, Warren, 118
Odd Fellows, 60

Odd Fellows lodge, 89, 128
Oden, James, 66
Oklahoma Territory, 50
Old Acre, 101, 102, 103, 129
Old Bob, (livery horse), 42
Old John (livery horse), 114
Old Memories, 53, 60
Old School, 126
Oldtown Inn, 45
Overseers of the Poor, 41
oxen, 21
oysters, 73, 112

—P—

Paeonian Springs, 23, 24, 42, 112, 114, 131
Page, George, 50
Page, Laura, 50
Page, Sam, 50
Palmer, John, 109
panthers, 16
Parker, Fred, 93, 134, 135
Parker, Harvey B., 87, 93, 134, 135
passenger pigeons, 88
Patrick Street, 47, 129
Patterson, Flemming, 28
Patterson, Nathaniel, 28
Paxson's Hall, 72, 131. *See* Town Hall
Paxson's Store, 76
Paxson, Ann Shawen, 66
Paxson, Burr W., 68, 70, 115
Paxson, Charles, 115
Paxson, Charles E., 93, 126
Paxson, John, 66
Paxson, Raymond (Piggy), 103
Paxson, William, 55, 58, 68
Peacock, Edgar, 117
Peacock, Francis O., 3, 117
Peacock, Will, 72

Phillips, Arthur Willis, 43
Phillips, Thomas, 20, 25, 35, 65
picnic woods, 123
Piedmont Cigarettes, 70
Pierpoint, Joseph, 55
Pierpoint, Margaret, 54
Pierpoint, Samuel, 54, 127
Pink House, 68
Point of Rocks, Maryland, 11, 21, 77, 86, 106
poll tax, 28
postmaster, 32, 45, 106, 113, 129
Potomac River, 12, 111
Potts, Jonas, 20, 98
pow-wowing, 36
Presbyterian manse, 123
Presbyterians, 8, 28, 89
Princeton University, 28
Purcellville, 114
Puritans, 17
Pusey, Joshua, 49, 64

—Q—

Quakers, 8, 12, 13, 14, 15, 17, 27, 38, 39, 40, 45, 119, 125, 127
quilting, 11

—R—

railroad, 21, 24
Ramey, Sanford, 38
Ramey, Sanford I., 49
Rankin, Thomas, 16
Ratcliffe, Mary, 127
Red Barn, 120
Reed, Amanda Smallwood, 53
Reed, Mary, 95
Reed, Oscar, 64
Religious Society of Friends. *See* Quakers
Respas, Billy, 89
Revolutionary Army, 18
Revolutionary War, 119
Rice, Thurza, 95

Richardson/Pierpoint/Ratcliffe house, 54
Rinker, Edward Franklin (Frank), 111, 112, 120
Ripple Bros., 72
Robinson, Nancy, 73
Robinson, Noble, 73
Robinson, William, 73
Rock Hall, 44
Rollison, Ebenezer "Ebbie", 8
Rosemont, 38
rough shoeing, 93
Round Hill, 130
Rucker, Clifton, 74
Rucker, Jim, 74
Rucker, Malinda, 74
Rucker, Nora, 74
Russell family, 129
Russell, Edmonia, 129
Russell, Henry, 49
Russell, Ida, 129
Russell, Minnie, 129
Russell, William, Sr., 39

—S—

Sally Nettle house, 52
Samuel Hough house, 109
sawmill, 99
scales, 23
school, 54, 72, 104, 117
School on Second Street, 97
Schooley's Mill, 99
Schooley, Ephraim, 64
Schooley, Heber, 68
Schooley, John, 99, 101, 102
Schooley, Mahlon, 108
Schooley, Milton, 99
Schooley, Rachel Louisa (Lucy) Steer, 13
Schooley, Reuben E., 101, 102, 127, 134
schools, 127, 128
Scotch-Irish, 28
Second Street, 29, 88, 97, 103, 123
Senator. The, 120
servitude, 40

Washington & Old Dominion Railroad, 23, 112
Washington, George, 98
Water Street, 40, 74, 87, 89
Waterford Academy, 128
Waterford Band, 114
Waterford chair, 64, 121
Waterford Fair, 23
Waterford Foundation, Inc., 4, 23, 85, 136
Waterford Market, 121, 131
Waterford News, 107
Waterford post office, 32, 53
Waterford School, 129, 130
Waterford, Ireland, 35
waterwheel, 23
Watson, Moses Pascal, 59
weavers, 47
Weavers Cottage, 38, 73
Webster, Fill [sic], 115
wells, 26, 27, 33
Wheatland, 44, 125
wheelwright, 101
wheelwright shop, 102, 134
White Lily flour, 23
White, Edward (Doc), 52, 72
White, Lt. Col. Elijah V., 68, 79, 106, 116
White, Robert J., 49
White, Sarah Janney, 13, 52
whitewashing & liming, 64
Williams family, 27
Williams, Abner, 63
Williams, Elizabeth Everett, 63
Williams, John, 51, 53, 62, 63, 105
Williams, Lydia, 105
Williams, Mary Elizabeth Walker, 52
Williams, Mrs. Mary Ruth, 32
Williams, Rebecca K., 115
Williams, William, 32, 44, 49, 51, 66, 74, 105, 127
Williams, William (the elder), 63
Wilson, Rev. W.H., 125
Winchester, Virginia, 27, 44
Wine, Daniel, Jr., 93
wolves, 16
Woman in Black, 86
Wood's mill, 93
woodstoves, 95
woodworkers, 88
woodworking shop, 89
World War II, 136
Worley, Hannah Mendenhall, 13, 104, 127
Wright, Edward S., 116
Wright, Jane, 27
Wright, Robert L., 49
Wright, William, 27

—Y—

Young, Henson, 39

Shawen family, 129
Shawen, Cornelius, 110, 129
Shawen, David, 110
Shawen, Mary, 110, 129
Sheridan, Gen. Philip, 59, 84
Simms, Jim, 36
singing, 51
Slater, Lt. Luther, 80
slaughterhouse, 97, 120
slavery, 38, 39, 40, 50, 59, 89
slaves, 47
sledding, 92
sleigh-riding, 93
Smith family, 50
Smith, Daniel G., 49
Smith, George D., 49
Smith, Lemuel P., 66, 75, 76, 77, 121
Snoots, Charles, 79
Snoots, William, 79
Society of Friends, 32, 44
Sons of Temperance, 60
spring houses, 94
Stabler, Edward, 36
stables, 21
Stahl, Edith, 85
Stanton, Edwin M., 35, 45
Star, Sunday, 42
Steer family, 27
Steer, Elizabeth Pancoast, 68
Steer, Franklin M., 134
Steer, Harriet Taylor, 109
Steer, Isaac, 48
Steer, James M., 68, 101, 103
Steer, Joseph, 102
Steer, Mary Frances (Mollie) Dutton, 53, 60, 134
Steer, Phebe Haviland, 3
Steer, Rachel, 13, 103
Steer, Samuel M., 105, 107
Steer, Sarah Ann, 107, 110, 127
Steer, William E. (Billy), 68

street lamps, 96
Sugar Shack, 51
suicide, 47
Sunday School picnics, 123
Sunnyside, 47, 106

—T—

Talbott Farm, 33, 81, 99, 123, 133
Talbott, Joseph, 99
Talbott, Joseph, Jr., 109
tank, 87, 92
tannery, 25
Tanyard Branch, 25, 43
tanyard, upper, 25
tanyards, 25, 35
Tate, William, 36, 59
Tavenner, Lot, 59
taverns, 60, 62, 72, 109, 127
Taylor family, 27
Taylor, Henry, 38
Taylor, Mary Ann, 109
Taylorstown, 80
teachers, 129
telephones, 51, 52, 53, 55, 62
Temple Hall, 44
tennis, 130
Thanksgiving, 112
thief, 76
Thompson, Amos, 28
threshing machine, 56
thunderstorms, 23, 72
Tin Shop, 112
tinners (roofers), 112
tithe, 28
tobacco, 111
Toleration Act, 28
Town Branch, 76, 88
Town Council, 63, 121
Town Hall, 70. *See* Paxson's Hall
town recorder, 113
town sergeant, 64
town spring, 89
Town Triangle, 87
Treaty of Albany, 12
Trough Hill (on Route 704), 123
turbine, water, 23

typhoid, 27, 34, 100, 108

—U—

undertaking shop, 97
Union of Churches Cemetery, 64, 118
Uwchlan Meeting, 27, 35

—V—

Vandevanter, Carrie Hough, 121
Vandevanter, Decatur, 108, 118, 121
Vandevanter, Joseph, 108
Vandevanter, Washington, 49
veterans, 119, 136
Virgin's Bower, 10
Virts, Charles W., 57
Virts, Henry, 126

—W—

Walker family, 27
Walker, Abel, 52
Walker, Cornelia, 127
Walker, Dan, 42
Walker, Edith (Miss Eed), 133
Walker, Elisha, 127
Walker, Eliza Hunt, 81
Walker, Isaac, 52
Walker, J. Edward, 109
Walker, Jacob, 32
Walker, James, 81
Walker, James M., 116, 127
Walker, Mary Branson, 52
Walker, Mrs. Jacob, 32
Walker, Nathan, 32, 49
Walker, Robert R., 127, 133
Walker, Susan, 81
Walker, Susannah Talbott, 52, 109
Walker, Violet (Vi), 42
War of 1812, 119

147